'It is time that Christians and men and women of good will rise up in unison, to declare the bedroom, like the boardroom and the trading floor, as the place of God's grace and celebration of humanity – not the place where women, children and men are sold into misery and degradation. I commend this book to all who wish to make a difference – thank you, Dawn.'
– Revd Dr Carrie Pemberton,
Founder Not for Sale UK, www.notforsalesundayuk.org

'Don't push these stories away. Allow them to touch you and motivate you. I pray that these stories and the larger picture Dawn offers will touch you as it has me.'
– Professor Scott Moreau, Wheaton College, Illinois

'Viewing the real face of prostitution has opened Dawn's eyes and caused her to take action. We hope that this book inspires the same reaction in you.'
– Mark and Josephine Wakeling,
National Christian Alliance on Prostitution (UK)

'I pray that Escaping the Devil's Bedroom will awaken the Christian community to the horror of prostitution and human trafficking, and motivate action to redeem those who are entrapped.'
– Revd Dr Lauran D. Bethell, American Baptist Churches

'Dawn presents the horror of this indescribable injustice in the context of hope. By seeing the Holy Spirit at work, we are inspired to move beyond awareness to action!'
– Dr Beth Grant, co-founder, Project Rescue International

Currently Publications and Training Manager at Media Associates International, Dawn Herzog Jewell has also worked for World Relief and the Billy Graham Center. She loves witnessing God's work in other cultures and has an MA in Intercultural Studies. She lives in Illinois with her husband Matt and young son Gabriel.

ESCAPING THE DEVIL'S BEDROOM

Sex trafficking, global prostitution
and the gospel's transforming power

Dawn Herzog Jewell

MONARCH
BOOKS

Oxford, UK & Grand Rapids, Michigan, USA

First published in the UK in 2008 by Monarch Books
(a publishing imprint of Lion Hudson plc),
Wilkinson House, Jordan Hill Road, Oxford OX2 8DR.
Tel: +44 (0)1865 302750   Fax: +44 (0)1865 302757
Email: monarch@lionhudson.com
www.lionhudson.com

ISBN: 978-1-85424-817-6 (UK)
ISBN: 978-0-8254-6165-1 (USA)

Distributed by:
UK: Marston Book Services Ltd, PO Box 269, Abingdon, Oxon OX14 4YN;
USA: Kregel Publications, PO Box 2607, Grand Rapids, Michigan 49501

Unless otherwise stated, Scripture quotations are taken from the Holy Bible, New International Version, © 1973, 1978, 1984 by the International Bible Society. Used by permission of Hodder & Stoughton Ltd. All rights reserved.

This book has been printed on paper and board independently certified as having come from sustainable forests.

British Library Cataloguing Data
A catalogue record for this book is available from
the British Library.

Printed and bound in Wales by Creative Print & Design.

To my father,
who gave me the gift of writing,
and my Uncle Cal,
who helped me discover it.

Contents

Acknowledgments

This book would not exist without the prayers and input of brothers and sisters in Asia, Africa, Europe, Latin America and North America. Nor could I have tackled it without the support of my boss, John D. Maust, and praying colleagues at Media Associates International (MAI). My publisher, Rodney Shepherd, and editor Tony Collins, at Monarch, believed in this project from its beginning.

Ministry leaders, staff, volunteers, and men and women free from sexual exploitation trusted me with their stories and introduced me to those they served. Leaders and staff of the National Christian Alliance on Prostitution in the UK guided me to deeper understanding of the issues. Multiple members of the International Christian Alliance on Prostitution (ICAP) were invaluable sources, as well as staff of the Salvation Army.

My church family at Church of the Resurrection (Wheaton, Illinois) accompanied me with their prayers and lent their insights, especially my prayer cell – Laura, Kate and Chloe.

Many people reviewed the manuscript or portions thereof and helped improve it with their suggestions – Miriam Adeney, Mindy Ashley, Sarah Aulie, Boaz Herzog, Philip Kenyon, Matthew Pechanio, Caryn Pederson, Jim Reapsome, Mark and Jo Wakeling. John Green and Jennifer Roemhildt lent their expertise to creating questions for the end of each chapter.

And others gifted me with their time and talents. Patrícia Croiter Evangelista shot photos in Brazil. Beth Johanson formatted and compiled photos. Eleni Tinga hosted me in Athens. Chloe Couch helped create my first blog. Mary Kiio interviewed her Nairobi neighbor. Ricardo Costa translated research from Portuguese. Anna Pugsley offered cover comments.

My husband, Matt, endured three weeks of remodeling chaos in our new home as I traveled in Europe doing research. Our unborn son, Gabriel, journeyed with me in his second trimester without any complaints. My parents and in-laws believed, with me, that this book was of God's leading.

God sent me the vision for this project, kicked me into action, urged me to believe, connected me with his people, and spurred me to its completion. I trusted sometimes in this verse he provided for the book's creation: 'Blessed is she who has believed that what the Lord has said to her will be accomplished!' (Luke 1:45).

Glossary of Terms

Customer, john, punter: Often used to describe the male buyers of commercial sex acts. A 'john' is a male purchaser in the US, also known as a 'punter' in the UK.[1]

Hustler: Used to describe a prostituted male in the US.

Madam: A woman who manages prostituted people.

Pimp: A pimp finds and manages clients for prostituted people and engages them in prostitution (in brothels in most cases, and in some cases street prostitution) in order to profit from their earnings.[2]

Prostituted or prostituting person: Terms used by those who view prostitution as a form of violence and exploitation rather than a voluntary 'job'. This phrasing avoids negatively labeling the person involved, while recognizing the activity of prostitution.[3] The term 'prostitute', however, equates prostitution with a person's identity.[4]

Prostitution: Provision of sexual favors in exchange for some form of payment, such as money, drink, drugs or even a bed for the night.[5]

Sex trafficking: The recruitment, harboring, transportation, provision, or obtaining of a person for the purpose of a commercial sex act.[6]

Sex tourism: Tourism partially or fully for the purpose of having or purchasing sex.[7]

Sex work/worker, sex industry: These terms may seek to legitimize prostitution as an occupation that any man or woman can freely choose. Although some people may choose it, there is likely far less choice involved than the terms convey for most prostituted men and women. Preferred terms include 'sexual exploitation' or 'commercial sexual exploitation'.[8]

Transgender: An umbrella term that can be used for all behaviour and thinking that crosses gender lines. Often applied to those who don't quite fit into the categories of 'transsexual' or 'transvestite'.[9]

Transsexual: An individual who seriously acts on the sense of having a body of the wrong gender, often but not always culminating in sexual reassignment surgery.[10]

Transvestite: People who cross-dress but do not consider themselves to be members of the opposite gender or do not desire to be.[11]

Trick: An act of prostitution or a person who pays for a commercial sex act.[12]

Foreword

Tragically, the world's oldest profession has one of the world's youngest workforces. Millions of preteen and teenage youth (girls and boys) are trapped in prostitution, typically earning money for their families or brothel owners. This global reality is far from the Hollywood fantasy foisted on the public through films like *Pretty Woman* (Julia Roberts) or *Hustle and Flow* (Terrence Howard).

The forced-labor aspect of much modern-day prostitution stands in stark contrast to efforts that misguided bureaucrats have undertaken to re-label prostitution as 'commercial sex work'. As a Salvation Army leader told me several years ago, 'Sex isn't work!' When sexual intimacy becomes a commercial service, the moral fabric of our culture is deeply damaged. Worldwide, hundreds of millions of people are damaged by the sex industry, pushing beyond our comprehension of evil. That's why we need writers such as Dawn Herzog Jewell to tell the stories of individuals. My finite mind can encounter and understand the story of one person, but not the stories of 100 million.

It is only with great difficulty that Christians and their churches decide to focus resources on fighting prostitution. Many of the ministry efforts today have emerged from para-church outreach. People who fight global prostitution yearn for more of God's people to be stirred deeply about the plight of mothers, daughters, sisters, sons, brothers, and cousins caught up in the sex trade. If no prostituted person is beyond the reach of God's grace, then no church or Christian can be exempt from concern and engagement on these issues at some level.

Many obstacles stand in our way. The demands of Christian ministry in our high-tech, 24/7 culture mean we live in a state of perpetual information overload. Adding yet another element to our already-overcrowded agenda seems impossible. There is also hostility in the news media, entertainment media, academia, the corporate world, and the public policy arena to traditional, biblical morality. Many powerful forces in our global society are too tolerant of sexual exploitation of the worst kind.

But God is always eager to work with the willing, and that should be the basis for our great hope. My strong prayer for this book is that it will open the eyes of Christian hearts, so that more of God's people would be willing. The first step is to see the prostituted woman as God sees her—a person first, made in His image. *Escaping the Devil's Bedroom* charts a new pathway of engagement.

Soli Deo Gloria.

Timothy C. Morgan
Deputy Managing Editor, *Christianity Today*

Introduction

When I began praying with my friend, Caryn, for a book topic to write about, I had no idea how God would answer my prayers. I have always enjoyed reporting on how God is working through the church around the world, building his kingdom brick by brick through visionary believers. In my daily work at Media Associates International (MAI), a Christian training agency for writers, editors and publishers, I opened emails from Kenya, Sri Lanka and elsewhere seeking advice on how to write and publish books about singleness in an African context, children's fiction for tsunami survivors, and so on. But without writing a book myself, I knew I was limited in my ability to encourage them.

A few months later when my husband, Matt, and I hosted a church missions event in our home, it wasn't because we felt called to reach women in prostitution. We wanted to rally our church to God's work overseas. But when Thelma Nambu of Samaritana, an outreach to prostituted women in the Philippines, described founding her ministry, I envisioned the stories of women from around the globe as chapters of a book. She talked about how, when sexually exploited people reach the point of willingness to tell their stories, that testimony can become part of the healing process. I heard God speaking to me, asking me to participate in their journey through telling their stories.

That was more than two years ago. Although Thelma and her husband, Jonathan, encouraged me to explore writing on the topic, I dragged my feet. My husband and I were both using our graduate degrees from Wheaton College, living in a quiet suburban neighborhood, and enjoying fellowship in a spirit-filled church. We ministered to an African refugee family, and my husband worked with children from multiple countries in his fifth-grade class. We were content. I had next to zero awareness of sexual exploitation, had never seen a red-light district, and felt miles away from the weight of this issue.

I knew that if I was ever to write this book, I needed to test the idea by writing a magazine article and getting feedback from skilled editors. But I did nothing for months. Then a writer friend told me that an editor at *Christianity Today* magazine had been seeking an article on outreach to women in prostitution for years. I felt like God had delivered me a swift kick in the rear.

Research for my article, 'Red-Light Rescue' (*Christianity Today*, January 2007) took me to the International Christian Conference on Prostitution in Wisconsin, where missionaries and indigenous leaders from more than thirty nations gathered to strategize, pray and exchange ideas. There I met many of the ministry leaders described in this book. I heard their prayers and God's desire to raise up more people with a heart for these broken men, women and children. I committed to writing this book there to show you how their stories have intersected with Jesus' followers. The result of these interactions, as you will read, has been eternal change for the kingdom.

In researching for this book, I visited ministries in Chicago, London, São Paulo, Manila, LA, London, Amsterdam and Athens. When I could not travel, I interviewed leaders, volunteers and survivors on their visits to the US, and by phone, email and Skype. You'll read about these modern-day heroes and prophets in the following pages. Their words are interspersed with my first-hand observations while visiting their ministries or conversations with them.

Learning at the feet of these dedicated men and women, I witnessed again and again how they lived out Jesus' love for 'the least of these'. Through them, I grasped that incarnational love is transformational.

When we hear of the millions of lives entangled in this ugly violence, it's easy to feel helpless. Media reports on sex trafficking and prostitution present numbing statistics on the vast network of this criminal trade in flesh. What can we do in the face of such a monumental evil?

My aim in writing this book is to reveal what today's headlines overlook. The Holy Spirit is at work in the dingiest alleys, streets and hotel rooms. Jesus' followers are reaching lives that the world, and sometimes the church, shuns and views as hopeless. These are the stories that shout to us that our God is greater than all other reality, power and authority.

In one of my first interviews, I was convicted when Mark Crawford (see Chapter 1) challenged me from Thailand: 'The issue is who wants them more. Do we, God's people, want these women and girls [and men] free more than the forces keeping them there?' That is the question I put before you in this book.

Mark used the phrase, 'the enemy's bedroom' to describe the darkness of sexual exploitation, and from that term, the title of this book came to me. The 'enemy' is the devil, who is thriving in the brothels, massage parlors, strip-clubs and bars where people are reduced to objects for sale. He grins each time sex becomes an impersonal financial transaction rather than God's gift designed only for the intimacy of marriage.

In the pages of this book, I hope you find that God's power is far greater than the snares of the devil's bedroom. The lives trapped in his harem are not hopelessly lost, nor are we help-less on the sidelines. Jesus offers new life to all, regardless of their chains and wounds. But without the resources of the global church, they will remain trapped. God is waiting for us to respond, so we can help bring more people into his trans-forming presence.

I do not attempt to offer a comprehensive overview of the issues, nor a handbook for how to do ministry. Other pub-lished resources offer in-depth research and analysis of people caught in prostitution and sex trafficking. The following pages aim to serve as an introduction to God's work among the sex-ually exploited in various corners of the world.

I have divided this book into three sections, inviting you to journey progressively with me and with the men and women who have escaped the suffering of the devil's bedroom and been restored in the light of the kingdom.

In Part 1, 'Stories of Darkness', meet men and women whose lives the devil has aimed to destroy. Through their sto-ries, gain glimpses into the painful past of survivors of sexual exploitation and their abusers.

In Part 2, 'Stories of Hope', follow the tracks of Jesus' fol-lowers –volunteers, ministry leaders, and staff – who are breaking society's taboos and patiently pursuing these lost men and women one by one. Read the testimonies of those who have escaped the devil's bedroom and discovered new life in Christ.

In Part 3, 'Your Part in the Story', consider how God might be calling you and your church community to make a differ-ence. Prayer, volunteering and advocacy are among the mul-tiple opportunities.

We'll explore questions like these in the following chap-ters: Do prostituted men struggle with certain issues? If a man or woman wants to leave the sex trade, what are their alternatives? Will an exotic dancer feel at home in a church? Can an unskilled, uneducated woman find a job that pays as well as prostitution? Why would a victim of trafficking become the perpetrator and want to traffic other women?

Throughout the book I use pseudonyms for men or women whom I've interviewed in order to protect their identities. When their stories are taken out of context, they can inadvertently serve as lasting labels that stigmatize, such as 'former prostitute'. But as their brothers and sisters, we want to embrace them as fellow sinners, equally redeemed. An asterisk after my first mention of a name indicates that this name is a pseudonym. A few volunteers or ministry staff have also asked for pseudonyms in order not to jeopardize the level of trust they've developed among the women and men they serve.

At the end of each chapter, take the time to go 'One step further'. Scripture passages, questions for reflection and suggestions for prayer offer opportunity to develop a biblical attitude toward sexually exploited people and outreach. They are intended for use either by individuals or by a group.

Please take warning that I have quoted several men and women who use offensive language at times. I have chosen to include these direct quotes because they best illustrate either painful circumstances or Jesus' unconditional acceptance of humanity. I hope that reading this dialogue helps increase your compassion.

This book is the product of prayers lifted from Asia, Africa, Europe, Latin America and North America. As you read, I invite you to join us in praying that the devil's bedroom would someday be empty. May we all see heaven overflowing with the men, women and children whose chains have been broken and whose scars are completely healed.

PART 1

Stories of Darkness

Chapter 1

The Battle Over the Devil's Bedroom

Today

Moon's* identity has changed from rescued to rescuer, from victim to counselor. She helps train others to work with victims of human trafficking and exploited street kids. Read more about Moon in Chapter 16.

Then

'I cursed every god. But in my heart, I believed someone would come and help me,' Moon says.[1]

When Moon was 12 weeks old in Myanmar (Burma), her birth mother sold her to a local woman, who raised her like a slave.[2] When Moon was 3 years old, this second 'mother' forced her to wash dishes in a restaurant eight hours a day.

When Moon turned 13, the woman sold Moon's virginity to a Western businessman in Thailand. But she fought her way free. A few months later, she wasn't so lucky. Her second 'mother' blocked the hotel room door after an Indian man paid 30,000 baht ($800) and then beat Moon with a belt until she submitted to sex. She had to be carried home. For ten days, Moon couldn't walk.

'I felt like throwing up,' she says. 'I was repulsed by my "mother" and afraid of men. I was sad and ashamed, because I wasn't clean.'

A year later, across the border in northern Thailand, the same woman tricked Moon into working at a noodle stand that was in reality a brothel. When Moon refused to comply with her first customer, the brothel owner slapped her and taped her hands to the bed. She shouted, so they forced a pingpong ball in her mouth and taped it shut. The second night, fifteen men used her; the next night, nine; the next, eleven. The 'customers' included men from Thailand, Myanmar, Japan, Korea, India and the West.

The owner's brother, a policeman, drugged Moon and ten other captive girls to keep them awake at night. They were threatened with cigarette burns. Moon tried to escape, but the owner and her brothers locked Moon in her room and kept an armed vigil at the brothel. Several times, policemen visited in street clothes and used Moon for free, compliments of the owner. She begged them for help. But they told the owner, who beat Moon and threatened to throw acid on her face. During her time in the brothel, given the average number of men who paid to use Moon each week, she was raped about 100 times.

Each year, millions of women, children and men are prostituted around the globe. Moon was one of an estimated 1 million children who annually enter the multibillion dollar industry of commercial sexual exploitation, according to UNICEF. In Thailand alone, where prostitution is technically illegal, some 200,000 girls and women are exploited each year.[3]

The global phenomenon of money-driven sexual exploitation is evident in the seedy strip-joints along US highways, the slum-and-brothel-lined streets of Calcutta, India, the fashionable sidestreets of London's Soho district, the busy street corners in São Paulo, Brazil, the canal-side window-fronts in Amsterdam and beyond. The stories of each woman, child or man may differ, but their wounded souls and scars of abuse are similar. Although not all are caged like Moon, they are all captive to the devil's lies that distort their sense of true identity.

The statistics are mind-numbing and the problem may appear hopeless. But Jesus didn't ask us to live comfortably and wait for his return. God seeks and saves that which is lost in the parables of the Lost Sheep, the Lost Coin and the Lost Son. God is the Shepherd who leaves the ninety-nine for the one; God is the woman who sweeps the house in search of the lost coin; and God is the Father who runs to the prodigal son. He asks us to do the same – to go in search of broken lives and invite them into the kingdom.

> He will rescue them from oppression and violence, for
> precious is their blood in his sight.   (Psalm 72:14)

Moon's cries were answered after nearly a month in the brothel. The Thai police and the International Justice Mission (IJM) rescued her after missionaries Mark and Christa Crawford had learned of her plight. Since then, the Crawfords have introduced Moon to Jesus and have tried to help her earn a decent living – a challenge for someone without marketable skills.[4]

Moon says that since the Crawfords entered her life, 'I have realized that I have value and worth. And now that I know God, I can always pray for his help whenever I have a problem.'

Today God continues to call out to society's forgotten through Jesus' followers. The Crawfords are among a growing number of Christians worldwide working to live out the love of Jesus by reaching out to sexually exploited people.

In 2001, the Crawfords relocated from Southern California to direct the Thailand office of International Justice Mission in the lush, mountainous city of Chiang Mai. They were drawn to move to Thailand after a short-term mission trip[5] to Asia. Christa, a graduate of Harvard Law School, was dissatisfied with corporate law and had been providing legal aid at the Union Gospel Mission in Los Angeles. Mark had been pastoring a growing multi-ethnic church while completing a master's degree at Fuller Theological Seminary; he was preparing himself to fulfill a call to minister to prostituting women.

When the couple began advocating through IJM for underage girls in forced prostitution, they noticed women over eighteen who were 'voluntarily' prostituting themselves. They lacked other viable options for supporting themselves and their families. Many women told Mark that they chose prostitution, but, he says, 'When you ask them what their choices were, they had only one choice.'

Thailand's neighbor to the north, Myanmar (Burma), has been under a military dictatorship for years, and its people have endured human rights abuses and a breakdown in the national economy. Consequently, an estimated 350,000 people have fled to Thailand, where they are considered illegal immigrants. Some 40,000 of these are women and girls exploited in Thailand's sex industry, many in Chiang Mai.[6]

The women the Crawfords talk to in bars, massage parlors and karaoke venues prostitute themselves to provide for parents and children. While it's normal for sons or daughters in Thailand to offer a portion of their income to parents or grandparents, Mark says families of prostituting women often demand 50 to 100 per cent of their daughter's income.

'Filial piety [respect and duty to parents] is an admirable Asian cultural value that's been perverted here by dysfunctional families and a changing society,' he says. The need for money leads women into the sex industry. They stay in prostitution because other available unskilled jobs pay significantly less.

Lisa Thompson, the Salvation Army's liaison for the abolition of sexual trafficking, says media attention on sex trafficking has 'captured people's hearts and [their] desire to help those perceived as poor, "innocent" victims' – those trapped in brothels, held at gunpoint, or locked in somebody's basement. 'But Christians tend to split prostituting women into two categories: the good prostitutes and the bad prostitutes. The good ones are victims of forced prostitution; the bad women are voluntary prostitutes and whores.'

'The problem is that women on street corners appear to be acting freely,' Lisa says. 'But passers-by are blind to the chains that bind women to prostitution: poverty, a lack of education, early drug use, a parent in prostitution, childhood sexual abuse, and the abusive tactics of traffickers and pimps.'

In a survey of prostituted men and women in nine countries including Thailand, the United States, Mexico, South Africa and Turkey, nearly nine out of ten said they longed to escape.[7]

But offering people freedom from prostitution requires more than just pulled heart-strings. 'The ministry of rehabilitation and healing is about stealing people from inside the enemy's bedroom, and he [the devil] says, "I own them",' Mark Crawford says.[8]

'The issue is who wants them more. Do we, God's people, want these women and girls [and men] free more than the forces keeping them there?'

Lifting the label

By Mark Wakeling, director of the National Christian Alliance on Prostitution, UK.

Consider the news headline, 'Prostitute Murdered'. In the media's rush to communicate the cruel death of a woman involved in prostitution, we read the stigmatizing label of 'prostitute'. This shorthand description implies that murder was a consequence of how the woman chose to live. But the label refuses us the opportunity to consider the person behind the label, created in the image of God and no different in value to any of us. Dignity was absent in life and is denied in death.

Stigmatizing labels not only overlook the inherent beauty and divine image of God's creation, they easily create in us a subtle and damaging attitude shift. When we choose to use a label we often separate ourselves from the people we have called 'prostitutes, johns, punters, pimps and madams'. Is this a healthy place to be? Is there a dividing line, or are we all deeply dependent on the grace of God? We may relish an ounce of security in creating this distance, but if we are honest, we have all failed and fall short of God's ways.

Alternatively, perhaps you agree that we should not label the victim, but only the guilty perpetrator – 'the john, trafficker, pimp or sex offender'. But if our ways are God's, we need to reconsider our language here also.

Recall Jesus' encounter with Zacchaeus (Luke 19:1–9). This chief tax collector voluntarily exploited others through financial dishonesty and oppression. Zacchaeus was much more an abuser than a victim. Yet to Jesus, he was still Zacchaeus, a man created in the image of God and desperate to recover his created identity.

The church is called to view people with Jesus' eyes rather than reinforcing society's stigmas, whether amongst victims or abusers of power in sexual exploitation. Both Jesus' followers and non-Christians are helping men, women and children caught in this awful trade of human misery. But ultimately, the people of God need to lead in communicating respect, offering dignity and recognizing God's value system by refusing to stigmatize people through careless labels.

Sex is a divine gift, and abuse of this gift results in physical, spiritual and emotional disease.

God was also abused, mutilated and publicly humiliated. He became vulnerable because he valued humans so much, including every woman, man and child in the sex trade. For us, Jesus entered into the world's darkness and the depths of our pain.

Today a steadily growing band of Jesus' disciples are breaking cultural taboos and following his footsteps around the globe. They are scouring red-light districts, seedy urban streets, smoky bars, and dark corners that are often neglected by churches.

In the parable of the Prodigal Son (Luke 15), the son stayed in a 'distant country' until he came to his senses and returned to his father's house. Ministries to men and women in prostitution go to that far-away land, rather than stay in the safety and Christian community of the 'father's house'. They help the prodigal come to his senses, point him toward the father's house, and walk with him along the way. Their aim is to remain in that distant country to seek the prodigals and help them come to their senses.[9]

This book will track Jesus' followers in that distant country and answer questions such as:

- Who are those still trapped?
- How did they fall captive in the devil's bedroom?
- What are their needs, hurts and hopes?
- Who are the faithful who are reaching one life at a time?
- What does effective outreach look like across cultures and contexts?
- What does life after commercial sexual exploitation look like?
- How can you help?

ONE STEP FURTHER

Read: If we are unconcerned about the poor, the lost and the forsaken, we will go to hell. Read Matthew 25:31–46.

Reflect: In light of this passage, how do you feel about the statement above?

Pray: That God will give you a heart of compassion for all men, women and children involved in commercial sexual exploitation.

CHAPTER 2

The Web of Deceit: Entangled in Sexual Exploitation

Today

I met Harmony Dust in LA at a Christian conference on sex trafficking. I quickly discovered she was an articulate speaker and a passionate advocate for churches as places of healing.

Harmony (age 31) is the founder and director of Treasures, an LA ministry that reaches women in the sex industry. Once a month, Harmony and a dozen or so young Christian women pile into a van and head to ten or more night-clubs across the sprawling city. They come bearing gifts to offer the dancers inside: bags of treats like lip-gloss and jewelry, with brochures that tell Harmony's story of meeting God while working as a stripper. Read more about Harmony's ministry in Chapter 10.

Then

Harmony thought she'd be dead by age 21. 'Suicide was a constant thought in my head. It wasn't a matter of if I was gonna kill myself, it was a matter of when,' she says.[1]

Harmony's parents had divorced when she was a toddler. Her mother struggled to provide for Harmony and her younger brother from their shabby cottage in Venice Beach, California. The family survived on welfare for months and, at other times, her mother sold crystals and handmade jewelry on the beach. Their financial uncertainties and her mother's gnawing cocaine habit made Harmony's life unpredictable.[2]

But it was the sexual abuse that caused Harmony's self-image to plummet over time. By the time she was a teenager, Harmony had been exposed to pornography at age 3, sexually abused by two women at age 5 or 6, again by an older boy at 7, and raped repeatedly as a teen by an ex-boyfriend. 'I hated myself for attracting slimy people. I felt such shame, I wanted to kill myself.'[3]

Harmony found solace in junior high school as an A student and vice-president of her class, but when she reached high school, she ran with the wrong crowd. She drank, smoked marijuana, shoplifted and neglected her grades. She and her mother fought frequently, and at 17 she fled home and spent a month in a group home for troubled kids. After she left, a psychologist she was referred to helped Harmony re-focus.[4]

Harmony enrolled in college and decided to major in psychology. But by then she had already given her body and soul to an older neighborhood boy. 'I had a really low sense of self-worth and my identity was strongly intertwined with my sexuality,' she told me.[5] At 15, she'd been giving him whatever money she had, and at 17 she had stolen money from the coffee shop where she worked as cashier. 'I thought that making him financially dependent on me was the only way I could make him stay, and I couldn't bear to be abandoned again.'[6]

Harmony lived with her boyfriend and supported him, and indirectly his baby and the baby's mother. At 19, she was more than $35,000 in credit-card debt. 'No matter how much I gave him, it was never enough. I was never enough and I felt undeserving of love.'[7] Even though her boyfriend started dating other women while they lived together, Harmony couldn't push herself to leave him.[8]

When a college classmate told her that stripping paid well, she decided to try it for a few months in order to pay off her bills. Her boyfriend thought the idea was fine. Instead of finding financial and personal freedom, she became trapped in the lifestyle.[9]

Harmony auditioned at the Century Lounge, a strip-club near the LA airport, in April 1996. The management hired her on the spot after she danced nude on stage to 'Purple Rain' by Prince.

Four nights a week, Harmony became 'Monique' at the club. She expected she'd be dancing in front of 'weirdos', but instead they were business travelers, executives, and regular guys frequenting the club after work.[10]

Other dancers caved in to pressure to sleep with regular customers, managers or club owners, but Harmony focused on the money from table dances. A dancer earned $15 a song (after the club took its $5 cut) to dance before a man at a small table behind a curtained cubicle. Since one song lasted less than four minutes, she could make $500 to $1,000 in one night, including good tips if she only took bathroom breaks.[11]

The men propositioned her nearly every night, but Harmony created firm boundaries – she'd never let a customer touch her, although many tried. Once she beat a man on the head with her heel when he licked her body as she was table dancing. She tipped a drink in another man's lap and punched his face after he yelled, 'Come here and bend over, bitch!' and cursed her again.[12]

Despite the money and attention from all the men, Harmony felt ugly and struggled with eating disorders. 'I was so unhappy. The pain was suffocating,' she said.[13]

The business of sexual exploitation takes many forms, including strip-clubs, street prostitution, massage parlors, brothels, escort services, lap dancing, phone sex, adult and child porn, child prostitution, video and Internet porn, trafficking and prostitution tourism.[14]

Inside the mushrooming numbers of strip-clubs and lap-dancing venues in the US and UK, intense emotional suffering, physical violence, and drug and alcohol abuse are common hazards for women on the job.

Strip-clubs in the US usually operate with legal business licenses, but many also offer forms of illegal prostitution to customers in back rooms. Similarly, massage parlors, saunas, health clubs, restaurants and bars may have such special rooms. Street prostitution is thought to comprise only 10 to 20 per cent of prostitution activities in the US.[15]

The website called the World Sex Guide details commercial sexual exploitation in countries around the world, with customers' latest ratings and descriptions of the women and their 'services'. Information posted about strip-joints in the Chicago area illustrates that some clubs offer nude dancing but 'no touching opportunities', while others have back rooms available at various prices for sexual activities. Similarly at another website that serves as a directory for strip-clubs, browsers read and leave reviews for clubs in hundreds of countries.[16]

The publisher of the 'Exotic Dancer Bulletin' estimates that 250,000 exotic dancers work in the US in some 2,500 strip-clubs, an increase of more than 30 per cent in the number of clubs since the late 1980s.[17]

In the UK, lap dancing is the fastest-growing sector of the British sex industry.[18] The first lap-dancing club opened in 1995, and in 2007, 150 legal clubs operated throughout the nation.[19]

Harmony's colleagues at the Century Lounge slept with managers or owners to obtain good shifts. The club owner once coerced Harmony to go on a date by threatening to take her off the shift. Another time he called Harmony and two other dancers off the floor. One dancer was crying. 'Did she happen to mention that she slept with me for $1,000? She's a f—ing whore,' he told them.[20]

Money was Harmony's objective in stripping, as she sacrificed her life and income for her boyfriend, giving everything in hopes of earning and keeping his 'love'. Looking back, she writes:

> In essence, my boyfriend became my pimp. Every night I came home and gave him all of my money. I had convinced myself that I didn't deserve it anyway. Whenever I did try to put aside money so that I could quit dancing, 'something' always came up and I would give him my savings. During one 'emergency', the nature of which he never told me, I handed him over $10,000 in cash.[21]

The majority of prostituted girls in the US don't view themselves as victims until years later. 'Instead, they often cling to the false belief they are doing what they want, that their pimp is the only one who can save them, that he will fulfill all his promises and that their lives will change.'[22]

Violence and abuse

Physical and verbal abuses are common to women exploited in strip-clubs, escort services and other prostitution venues. The abuse experienced by women in strip-club prostitution includes 'being grabbed on the breasts, buttocks and genitals, as well as being kicked, bitten, slapped, spit on, and penetrated vaginally and anally during lap dancing.'[23]

In a Chicago survey, one in five women in escort services said they'd been raped more than ten times, the same percentage as women prostituting on the street. Fourteen per cent of women stripping said they'd been raped more than five times.[24]

The bridge from child sexual abuse to the abuse inherent in commercial exploitation is not far, as Harmony says: 'From my earliest memory I had been sexualized. It was almost training for becoming a stripper – I was used to being objectified.'[25] She adds: 'My view of the world was tarnished. I couldn't go anywhere without thinking that people saw me in a sexual way. I felt reduced to an object and in real life, I tried to hide behind baggy clothes and glasses.'[26]

Although Harmony decided not to prostitute, her work as a stripper was a form of commercial sexual exploitation that gradually overshadowed her true identity. Loss of personal identity is common for people in prostitution. Researchers compare them to slaves and concentration-camp prisoners who become 'what masters, Nazis or customers want them to be'.[27]

Half blasted to cope

To cope with the degradation and damaging environment, drug and alcohol dependence is common for women in both indoor venues like strip-clubs and street prostitution. A former stripper and prostitution survivor, Olivia began stripping at 16 in Chicago's Rush Street, attracted by the attention, money and glamour. She imbibed increasing amounts of alcohol to dull her senses, take her clothing off and then to prostitute in the club's back rooms.

'You learn to put up with a few things, and every time you do an act, it better prepares you to do a little bit more next time. You kind of desensitize yourself to what is really happening, and you are using more and more alcohol. I soon knew what the guys were looking for, and it didn't take long to figure out the scene. How did I do it? I was always in an altered state of mind before I got there. I came in drunk. I'd be half blasted before I arrived.'[28]

In another Chicago study, four of five women in stripping said they used drugs more frequently or more drugs more often than before they began.[29] Marijuana was the most common drug of choice that dancers used to relax themselves as an alternative to alcohol.[30]

Proud to be whores?

Despite the abusive environments they work in, some women choose to remain in stripping because it pays the mortgage, supports their children or provides the disposable income they desire for expensive clothes, jewelry and more. And some women say they love the job because it enables them to take control of their sexuality.

At a 2006 conference in Las Vegas, strippers, prostituted men and women, and activists lobbied for legalized prostitution and better treatment by law enforcement. 'We're proud to be whores. There's safety in numbers. We're not afraid. We're not going to take this [treatment by law enforcement] anymore,' said Robyn Few, executive director of Sex Workers Outreach Project USA.[31]

The week-long conference for 'sex worker rights' drew about 150 people from different countries and organizations. Proponents of 'sex work' – prostitution, stripping, porn, topless waitressing – say it's a career choice. Many call themselves feminists and say society should face the reality that sex is a legitimate commodity that sells products globally.[32]

'[Prostitution is] probably the most honest relationship there is between a man and a woman,' says Susan Lopez, a former stripper and the assistant director of the Desiree Alliance, a national network of non-profit sex-worker rights organizations.[33]

She is unashamed of her own background and wants to encourage other women. 'What I want to do with my work with sex workers [is] to lift them up as goddesses and not below men. They're equal with men,' Lopez says. 'You got the pussy! You've got the gold! You've got the power!'[34]

There is no single profile for a woman who endures commercial sexual exploitation, although many come from abusive pasts. Harmony's friends at the club had varied backgrounds.

'They were aspiring actresses, students and single moms,' she says. 'Some were drug or alcohol addicts; others used drugs just to help them get through a shift at work. Most of the girls had given up their ambitions outside of stripping. One woman had a beautiful voice, but her boyfriend started beating her, so she forgot about her dream of having a singing career. My friends were not happy women.'[35]

'A lot of them are carrying around a lot of hurt and anger, crying in the dressing rooms,' she says. 'There was one girl who every night would cry huddled in the corner, then wipe her tears and get on stage. Then go back to the dressing room and cry again.'[36]

ONE STEP FURTHER

Read: Psalm 8:3–5:

When I consider your heavens, the work of your fingers, the moon and the stars, which you have set in place, what is man that you are mindful of him, the son of man that you care for him? You made him a little lower than the heavenly beings and crowned him with glory and honor.

Reflect:
- Do you see the prostituted woman or stripper as crowned with glory and honor? What about bar owners or customers? Are they made a little lower than the angels too?
- If we look at someone as repulsive, does it show something equally repulsive within us?
- How does God view people?

Pray: For eyes that see people as God does.

CHAPTER 3

Cycles of Abuse and 'Sex Tourism'

Today

Ana* (age 31) is reaching children for Christ. She teaches Sunday school and helps with her church's monthly street evangelism outreaches. She dreams of going to Africa to share Jesus' love with street children.

I met Ana on her first visit to the US at an international conference in rural Wisconsin. She told her story there, then shared more details with me in private.[1] She wanted more people to know the power of God to save from the pit of despair. Read more about Ana today in Chapter 17.

Then

Ana grew up in rural Costa Rica, far from the bustling capital of San José. The eldest of five sisters and one brother, Ana parented her siblings while her parents neglected them. The family couldn't afford to send the children to school. While mother and father served as pastors in a local church, they entrusted their children for long hours with members of the worship team. But these church members sexually abused

Ana and her sisters. First at age 6, and until she was 15, Ana was molested multiple times.

As the eldest child, Ana was responsible for feeding her siblings, but basic necessities were often scarce. When she was only 7, Ana's grandfather blackmailed her, requesting sexual favors in exchange for food. 'It was okay for him to abuse me but not my little 4- and 5-year-old sisters,' she says. Ana relented in order to help put food on the table and protect her younger sisters.

Ana kept all the abuse a secret, but her face bore the trauma. 'I had facial paralysis on the right side because I was so stressed out,' she says. She hoped her parents would notice, but they never did. 'I was never able to speak out, but something inside me was yelling, "Help me!"'

Her parents turned away from the Lord and their marriage disintegrated when Ana was 12. She witnessed her father walk out on her mother and abandon the whole family. 'I saw my mom begging him, "Please don't leave me."' She was three months pregnant.'

That day Ana promised herself she'd never cry for a man or let anyone abandon her. She decided men were evil. That year Ana started taking drugs to numb the pain.

After her husband left, Ana's mother dated other men, and many came to live with the family. The boyfriends often wanted to have sex with Ana's sisters. If a girl didn't cooperate, her mother kicked her out of the home. Once at a party, Ana's mother offered her 14 and 15-year-old daughters to a man for sex. When he came to the house, the girls refused. It wasn't the only time their mother tried to sell the girls for sex.

When Ana turned 18, she left home and family behind. But the tourist center where she thought she'd be working as a waitress turned out to be a brothel. Ana soon started selling her body, then drinking and using drugs to alleviate her suffering.

Although Ana knew she was sinking into darkness, she was also aware of God whispering in her ear. 'I knew God was calling me, but I didn't want to follow him because I thought he was cruel and had abandoned me,' she says.

Ana's story of poverty, neglect, abuse and incest is not unusual for prostituted women. The deep scars of early sexual abuse can lead to a downward cycle of more abuse in prostitution. Cultural attitudes toward females, low education levels and poverty also contribute to the vulnerability of women and girls to sexual exploitation. These factors, combined with men seeking paid sex, create fertile soil for 'sex tourism' and the sexual abuse of children by wealthy customers from abroad.

Sexual abuse and incest

The ongoing sexual abuse and incest that Ana endured paved the way for her to begin prostitution. Prolonged and repeated trauma usually precedes entry into prostitution. Among prostituted people in 9 countries, 63 per cent reported child sexual abuse, although researchers place the actual figure closer to 85 per cent, since traumatized people tend to minimize their experiences.[2]

Like prostituted adults, incested children are bribed by adults into sex and offered food, money or protection in exchange for their silence.[3] The psychological symptoms resulting from incest and prostitution are similar – such as depression, substance abuse, anxiety disorders and post-traumatic stress disorder. Among prostituted women, depression is common.[4]

One woman began prostituting after realizing she had been sexually abused as a child: 'there was no sense of having a life; the only life I knew of was prostituting... I thought I couldn't be hurt no more and I felt that I could do what I want and could have sex with whoever I want because somebody had already gone and messed my system up.'[5]

Prostitution can be a way for sexual abuse victims to try and gain control over their past. When Ana witnessed her father walk out, she determined to throw out and abandon men instead of being victimized. Later, when she began prostituting, she may have attempted to take control over her sexuality, which men had already exploited.

Unfortunately, the cycle of abuse continues both physically and mentally. Researcher Melissa Farley says, 'Prostitution keeps alive the experience and dynamic of child sexual abuse for the prostituted girl or woman.' They describe flashbacks to incest or molestation during acts of prostitution.[6]

Supply and demand:
The powerless and the powerful

If viewed as a market, prostitution and sex trafficking include forces of both supply and demand. On the supply side, poverty, corruption, lack of education, unemployment and the desire to improve one's life make powerless people vulnerable to commercial sexual exploitation. These are considered 'push factors'.[7]

The forces of market demand and the power-holders – especially men seeking to purchase sex – create incentives for men involved in pimping, brothel and strip-club owners, and people involved in trafficking to lure more victims, fueling the rise of sex trafficking and increasing venues for prostitution. These are 'pull factors'.[8]

The market demand for prostitution in Latin America, and particularly Costa Rica, has risen in recent years. Latin

America now ranks with Asia as one of the two most active regions in the world for the criminal sexual exploitation of women and children.[9]

Poverty is a significant 'push factor' for women entering prostitution around the world. In Costa Rica, more than 27 per cent of the people live in poverty – a condition that frequently drives the market for children, who can bring in large sums of money at little cost to their pimps.[10] The need for money results in families 'pimping' their children and leads women into the sex industry.

Ana's parents' inability to provide for their children's basic needs contributed first to the incest that she endured, and eventually to her prostituting. Her lack of an elementary education also limited her economic options.

Women and children are particularly vulnerable to poverty, with women comprising nearly three out of four of the world's 1.5 billion poor people.[11] The web of poverty keeps women disproportionately disadvantaged, undereducated and discriminated against.

In many cultures and religions, women and girls are valued less than males. This devaluation contributes to their poverty and vulnerability to sexual exploitation. In Latin American culture, *machismo*, a male code of honor and conduct (especially in rural areas), at its worst, can legitimize the domestic abuse of women and their open sexual exploitation in the workplace and on the street.[12]

Child sex tourism

With the ease of international air travel, arranging sex 'tourism' – including sex with under-age girls – is almost as simple as clicking on a website. By taking trips to areas where prostitution thrives, tourists or business travelers can easily take advantage of the estimated 2 million prostituted children in Asia, Latin America and Africa. Economically depressed or politically unstable regions are especially vulnerable to commercialized sex.[13]

According to World Vision, some predators travel specifically for 'sex tours', expecting anonymity, low-cost prostitution, ready access to children, and immunity from prosecution. Americans account for 25 per cent of child sex tourists, according to reliable global estimates.

The average victim is 14 years old, although some prostituted children are pre-adolescent. Besides the emotional and physical wounds of sexual abuse, the children are also at great risk of HIV infection.[14]

Costa Rica has more than 300 brothels in San Jose alone,[15] and may rival Thailand and the Philippines as one of the world's leading destinations for prostitution tourism.[16] Among others, the industry serves thousands of North Americans who travel to Costa Rica each year as 'sex tourists'.[17]

As Central America's leading tourist destination, Costa Rica is also believed to have the region's largest child prostitution problem.[18] Commercial sexual exploitation of children in Costa Rica could involve as many as 5,000 sex 'tourists' every year.[19]

The Costa Rican government has increased its commitment to help stop sexual exploitation in recent years by granting funds to aid organizations such as Rahab Foundation, a Christian group that helps women who have left prostitution rebuild their lives.[20] Campaigns against child sex tourism continue, in addition to TV, radio and billboard notices to warn young women of the danger of commercial sexual exploitation.[21]

Internationally, prosecutions are rare, whether due to lack of laws or corrupt law enforcement. In a recent case, Australian police arrested a pilot, charging him under an anti-sex tourism law. He is accused of abducting a Papua New Guinea girl and forcing her to have sex with him.[22]

To combat child sex tourism, World Vision has teamed up with national governments and US immigration and law enforcement agencies. US citizens and residents can face up to 30 years' imprisonment for engaging in sexual activity with children under 18, even if they do so outside the US.[23]

Sadly, corrupt law enforcement feeds the problem in countries such as Thailand, says Graham Tardif, who until recently oversaw World Vision's anti-trafficking program in Thailand. Since trafficking profits are huge and local wages are low, accepting bribes to look the other way is a huge temptation for police and immigration officers, despite government attempts to end such corruption.[24]

In addition to encouraging proper law enforcement, World Vision is sponsoring a media campaign to dissuade potential child sex tourists. It includes airport billboards and posters, ads in tourist magazines, in-flight video announcements, and brochures in taxis and hotels in Costa Rica, Thailand, Cambodia, Mexico and the United States.[25]

But the problem remains massive. In Thailand alone, the government-sponsored Baan Kredtakarn center in Bangkok has been providing shelter and assistance for women and girls for more than 40 years. World Vision's Tardif estimates that more than 90 per cent of the girls treated there are victims of child sex tourism and trafficking. That is not likely to be an exaggeration, considering that the Thai government admits there are 20,000 to 30,000 children involved in its commercial sex industry.[26]

ONE STEP FURTHER

Read: John 4:1–42. Jesus' encounter with the Samaritan woman at the well captures God's transforming power in the lives of his most broken and alienated children. Before meeting Jesus, this nameless woman endured daily discrimination and her neighbors' disdain because of her reputation and life history. Despite Jewish cultural taboos, Jesus entered Samaria at hot noontime and met this stigmatized woman by the well.

At that time, Jewish men were not supposed to mingle with women in public, nor were the religious to relate with 'unclean' persons. Mesmerized by her brief but radical encounter with Jesus, the Samaritan woman's deepest thirst was quenched by Jesus' offer of Living Water. She was liberated and forgot her jar, running to her neighbors to tell them about Jesus. Her testimony led people in her town to seek Jesus and experience the new life she had testified about and received.[27]

Reflect: Can you think of ways that your society values girls and boys differently?

What might have been done to help Ana and her family earlier in her story? Do you know of any troubled families like Ana's in your community? Ask God what he might want you or your church to do to help.

Pray: For women and girls in your community to know the value they have before God. Pray also for women and girls in other cultures who are vulnerable to abuse and exploitation because of society's mistaken ideas about their worth.

CHAPTER 4

Men in Prostitution: Equal Opportunity, Equal Despair

Today

Up to a point I really thought I was protecting myself –
whether with a gun, a stick or how well I could fight…
Now I can barely walk 2 blocks without having to stop
and sit down… I know I'm not protecting myself now,
it's God.[1]   Andy*

I first met Andy in the softly-lit basement chapel of Emmaus
Ministries' drop-in center in Uptown Chicago. We were in a
men's Bible study group. He was candid about his struggles
and agreed to talk with me later by phone. Read more about
Andy today in Chapter 11.

Then

When a gnawing crack addiction engulfed Andy's life almost
two decades ago, he abandoned family and friends. He was
sleeping on park benches in Chicago's exclusive Gold Coast
area when another homeless man suggested he earn an easy
$250 from a car that sidled to the curb. To feed the drug habit,

Andy gave it a try and began selling his body to mostly gay men at night.[2]

'It gave me a false sense of feeling good about myself,' he says. 'Guys driving around in big, nice cars, staring at me and wanting to pay for my services... I wouldn't feel so ugly when they picked me up. Before I'd feel like the ugliest thing in the world – the ugly, homeless drug addict.'[3]

Andy once ran a successful barber business on Chicago's south side. He enjoyed the gang members who crowded his basement, waiting their turn. But when he began snorting crack, 'It took me for a different spin,' he says.[4]

Andy's mother had taken him to church as a child, and her girlfriends prayed for him. 'The older women in the church would say, "Where's my baby, Andy? He's gonna be a pastor one day,"' he recalls. But for years, the seeds of the gospel seemed to land on concrete.[5]

Hooked on crack, Andy sold his cars and barber tools for the narcotic. He missed a chance to go on tour cutting hair for New Edition, a popular R&B band.[6] 'I left the neighborhood and went to the Loop, 'cause I needed someplace to get out of the shame and guilt spotlight.' In despair, Andy soon began prostituting.[7]

In the early nineties, Andy was diagnosed with AIDS. 'I felt like I just murdered so many people,' he says. The jolt motivated him to squelch the booze and crack habit, and he started going to church again and attending AA meetings. But a relationship with a woman distracted him from God and the AA visits. He fathered twins, but Child and Family Services took the two from him. 'I used that as an excuse to start back on drugs,' he says.[8]

Andy vainly continues to numb the pain in his life with alcohol and drugs. His body is falling apart. 'I can smell an acid smell from my body. I can shower, wash my clothes, but I still smell it. My body is dying but I'm still alive.'[9]

Prostitution includes the sexual exploitation of both men and women. They often bear similar backgrounds of abuse and endure violence by customers. Transgendered people are among the most marginalized of prostituted men and women, and are often rejected by society on first glance.

Male prostitution is a hidden but rising trend in American cities. Men comprised four in ten prostitution arrests in 1998, more than double what the FBI reported in 1970. In Chicago, police arrest about 3,000 men a year for prostitution and 5,000 women. Emmaus Ministries founder, John Green, attributes this increase to the growing gay community and the continuing breakdown of families.[10]

Surprisingly, prostituting men are usually not gay, John says.[11] 'So many of our guys have huge starving holes for a father.' By the time a man begins prostituting, he is bearing immense pain. 'Most guys have been sexually abused, the majority are high school or middle school drop-outs, and most don't know who their fathers are.'[12]

'They're looking for everything we are – a place to call home, love and acceptance in the world. But the streets twist those things,' John says. 'Every voice speaking into their lives is negative and dark.'[13]

The experiences of men, boys and transgendered people in prostitution are similar to those of women and girls. Ninety-one per cent of prostituting men said they wanted to escape prostitution in a study in Washington DC.[14] Levels of post-traumatic stress disorder were the same among men, women and transsexuals in prostitution in the US, Thailand and South Africa.[15]

Physical violence is also a common experience for males in prostitution, whether resulting from abusive customers or homophobic men. Andy says, 'There were guys who'd drive up in a Chevy van. After a while I got to know who they were – four or five in the back and one guy in the front who posed as a john. You get in the van and he'd drive you off to a secluded area and they'd just take turns kickin' your butt.'[16]

Samuel, another guest at Emmaus Ministries, says, 'I had my share of – we used to refer to them as "bad tricks". There was this one time, at 915 West Wilson Street, right next door to Emmaus. There was this guy – he and I were up at his house getting high, and he had a bad trip. And this guy hit me in the head with a pipe and threw me out of a fourth-floor window.'[17]

Many men who stay on the streets are killed prematurely by violence, drugs or illness. About one in three prostituting men who visit Emmaus are HIV-positive, John Green says.[18]

The very least of these

Transgendered people comprise a significant minority of people in prostitution in the US and internationally.[19] They are often the most marginalized among prostituting men and women. Shunned by society, they may encounter difficulties finding regular employment. In Chicago, transvestites command more money prostituting. Married men with homosexual desires may want to engage a transvestite because, 'He justifies he's out with a woman although the genitalia is a man's', says Sil Davis, ministry director of Emmaus Ministries.[20]

In São Paulo, Brazil, Latin America's largest metropolis, there are an estimated 2,500 transvestites and transsexuals, according to Paolo Cappelletti, former director of CENA ministries.[21] Homosexuality is widely tolerated in Brazil, where the 2007 'Gay Pride Parade' attracted some 3 to 4 million supporters, making it the world's most attended street event.[22]

In one São Paulo neighborhood I saw sidewalks lined with transsexuals soliciting customers – flaunting mini-skirts, baring breast implants and turning heavily made-up faces at passing cars. New transgendered people can earn up to $1,500 US a month.[23] Roberto used to number among the transvestites, hoping to turn a trick to pay for his next high.

As a child, Roberto* felt different from other Brazilian boys. When he was only 13, Roberto's father kicked him out of the family's house: 'If you're a homosexual, I don't want you living with us.' Homeless, Roberto tried to earn a living as a houseboy, cleaning homes around the country and living wherever he could find work.[24]

At 15, he decided to become a transvestite and aimed to save money for sex-change surgery. When he arrived in São Paolo at 21 years old, he began snorting crack daily and prostituting himself as a transvestite to earn money for his next high.[25]

Roberto's estrangement from his family was not unique. Other gay or bisexual men leave home because of their family's response to their sexuality. Often young and poorly educated, one of their limited economic options is commercial sexual exploitation. And like Roberto, 'because gay and bisexual men are defined by both society and the gay community itself in sexual terms, many of these young men come to view themselves exclusively in sexual terms.'[26]

Read more about Roberto in Chapter 12.

ONE STEP FURTHER

Read: Luke 15:11–32, the prodigal son.

Reflect: Men in prostitution are often like the prodigal son, separated from their families, alone and wandering far from home. Society rejects them. Will we?

Pray: Confess any disgust you may feel about male prostitution. Ask God to lead more people to reach men on the streets and strengthen those already about God's business.

CHAPTER 5

Modern-day Slavery:
Sex Trafficking

I hailed a cab to the office of Scarlet Cord, an outreach to prostituted and trafficked women in Amsterdam's famous red-light district.[1] The cab driver couldn't find the address, so he dropped me off with vague instructions and left me to find it on my own. I inquired in a 'coffee shop' that smelled like marijuana before stumbling on the narrow street myself. Red neon lights hung above windows just past the Scarlet Cord's humble entrance. Jesus' followers were located in the center of the devil's bedroom.

Later on that drizzling Monday night, I walked along lantern-lit cobble-stone streets and canals in the red-light district. Although it was a weekday after 9 p.m., the streets were filled with throngs of passers-by ogling at the scantily-clad young women who stood in the windows as if they were animals at the zoo. After my initial shock at the women's 'come-hither' poses and their heavily painted faces, I began noticing the onlookers. They weren't only leering and lusty young men who stopped to window-shop. Couples strolled hand-in-hand and grandfatherly and grandmotherly figures took in the 'sights'. Apart from the absence of children, all of humanity seemed to be out for a stroll in the city's central red-light district.

Then I realized that my picture of the zoo was inside-out. In fact, it was we on the streets, the people strolling by, who were more the animals, feeding fallen appetites for bizarre spectacles and fantasy on the women behind the windows.

I was accompanied by Toos, who oversees the Scarlet Cord (*Scharlaken Koord* in Dutch) with her husband, Willem. She tapped on windows and doors, introducing herself with a friendly hello and letting the women know they were welcome at the Scarlet Cord if they ever needed help. The first door we knocked at was opened by a young Hungarian girl who looked younger than 20 and spoke only a little Dutch. Unlike the other women, her freckled face bore little if any make-up, and instead of cheap lingerie, she wore a modest white-and-silver polka-dot swimsuit. She said her name was 'Lucy'.

I'll never know Lucy's story, but I am confident she didn't grow up dreaming of becoming an object in the window. More likely, she's one of many young women who fit a common profile. Perhaps her father was an alcoholic or abusive, then her mother became sick and needed hospitalization or medication. With younger siblings at home, and few local job prospects, Lucy enlisted to work abroad as an 'exotic dancer' or 'nanny'. Or maybe she even knew she'd 'work' in a window, but she probably imagined earning piles of money to send back home for her family. She never fathomed the violence and suffering almost certain to come.

The relationship of prostitution and sex trafficking is tightly woven, not simply defined by whether a person 'chooses' to engage in sexual exploitation. Without demand for prostitution, sex trafficking would not exist. The crime of sex trafficking includes the use of brutal control tactics and flagrant lies to seduce vulnerable women and girls. The prostituted person is deceived, abused and deprived of human dignity.

In the Netherlands, where prostitution was legalized in 2000, commercial sexual exploitation generates an estimated $1 billion nearly each year.[2] It is a major destination for trafficked women; its 2,000 brothels and many escort services use some 30,000 women.[3] As many as 80 percent of the women are estimated to be from other countries.[4] In one Amsterdam study, 79 per cent of prostituted women said they were in prostitution due to a degree of force.[5]

Human trafficking is the third largest criminal industry in the world, after arms and drug dealing. It is also the fastest growing, with millions of victims trafficked from 127 countries worldwide and extensive profits.[6]

Of the estimated 600,000 to 800,000 people trafficked across international borders annually, 80 per cent of victims are female, and up to 50 per cent are minors. Hundreds of thousands of these women and children are used in prostitution each year. These figures don't include the many people trafficked within their own countries.[7]

Demand for trafficked women is often highest in countries where women enjoy a high status and relatively few engage in commercial sexual exploitation.[8] Commercial sex businesses in the West – the US, the UK, Canada, the Netherlands, Germany, Austria and Australia – are filled with women trafficked from Asia, Africa, Latin America and Eastern Europe. Half of prostituted women in Germany were found to be illegal immigrants.[9]

Big business

Sex trafficking is a multi-billion-dollar market. Women are trafficked to, from, and through every region in the world using methods that have become new forms of slavery.[10] The sex trade in women is highly profitable and relatively low risk compared to trade in drugs or arms. Women's bodies can be sold and used repeatedly, unlike drugs or arms. And women and girls are vulnerable to trafficking tactics because they are often disproportionately poor, disadvantaged, less educated and discriminated against.

UK trafficking

In the UK, the sex industry has an annual value of £770 million.[11] In London alone, men spend £200 million a year on buying sex, half in massage parlors and saunas.[12]

Seduced by the financial gains to be made, a man pimping a number of girls can earn up to £6,000 per week, and a person trafficking compliant females can earn up to £120,000 per annum.[13]

Trafficking victims may be bought and sold for between £500 to £8,000, with an average estimated price of £2,000 to £3,000.[14]

In 2003, up to 4,000 women had been trafficked in the UK for sexual exploitation. British authorities rescued 84 victims during 4 months in 2006, predominantly from Eastern Europe, China/South-east Asia, Africa and Brazil.[15]

Seduction

People who traffick lure victims with jobs offering an escape from grinding poverty or instability in their own countries, and a chance for success and relative wealth. Newspaper ads placed by bogus recruiters and employment agencies solicit nannies, waitresses, models and maids. Few or no qualifications are required, and they typically advertise for young, single women.

One ad in a Kiev newspaper read, 'Girls: Must be single and very pretty. Young and tall. We invite you for work as models, secretaries, dancers, choreographers, gymnasts. Housing is supplied. Foreign posts available. Must apply in person.' The majority of these jobs do not exist.[16]

Not all women are seduced by phony job ads. Many women are recruited by a relative, neighbor, or friend of a friend who takes advantage of a trusted relationship and offers to help the woman get a job abroad. Other tactics include flagrant abduction, men posing as 'boyfriends', match-making services for 'mail-order brides', and the use of trafficked women whose 'managers' offer them a trip home with flashy jewelry and nice clothes to attract new victims with tales of life in the wealthy West.[17]

Control tactics

Men involved in pimping, trafficking and battering women use common methods of coercion to 'season' women into fear and submission. Ultimately, their goal is to obtain complete control over the women and to ensure that they are 'too terrified and too psychologically and physically broken down to contemplate escape'.[18]

In the US, more than 90 per cent of prostituted women are estimated to be under the control of pimps.[19] One website advertises the 'Pimp Easy Book: The Complete Step-by-Step Instructional Manual'. The author promises to lead 'you step-by-step, from how to get a female, conditioning her mind (and body), and if you like, getting her to the street (strip-club, escort, Internet, or track) or simply getting control over her.'[20]

A man intending to pimp typically establishes a relationship with the woman or girl he wants to prostitute. He calls himself her boyfriend or promises marriage, creating a relationship of connection and ownership that enables him to gain trust and begin the coercion process.[21] The tactics he uses to break the woman down emotionally, psychologically and physically include battering, starvation, rape, verbal abuse and telling her she's good for nothing but sex.[22]

One woman said: 'They told me they would cut me into pieces and send me back like that. Every single day I heard the threat, "I'll kill you, bitch."'[23]

These men may isolate a prostituted woman and keep her from getting other jobs. They often will not let her out of sight, watching her from across the street or following her to the emergency room after beating her. They aim to control the woman's sense of identity, including changing her name or appearance. They reinforce the idea that they own the woman and have created her for the purpose of prostitution.[24]

Like battered women, prostituted women become dependent on and controlled by their abusers. If they try to leave, they may face beatings, rape, threats of murder and more.[25]

Coercion by voodoo

Nigerian women from Edo state are frequent trafficking victims in Western Europe. Grace was trafficked to Amsterdam, propelled by the belief that prostitution would make her quickly wealthy and enable her to support her ailing mother. She describes the voodoo rituals she was required to undergo before leaving Nigeria:[26]

'During the Oath you give some evidence to the priest. This is a package of physical material from your own body. The cost of breaking my promise to Nora was high: my life and my happiness. Should I, for whatever reason, not meet my obligations, then Nora would call in the ju-ju priest. He would have my physical material, with which he was able to curse or manipulate me with occult powers...

'The priest put raw liver in front of me, which I had to eat. After that, a piece of raw heart – which I flushed down with a gulp of gin. I had to take off my clothes. The priest wanted to take my knickers. He would keep them with the rest of my material in his possession. He took hairs off my head and also some pubic hair. He made small scars on my arms and between my breasts. A mix of powder and poison was rubbed into them, while he spoke all kinds of magic words and made strange sounds. This would protect me against dangers like the police, and also against diseases. He also put pieces of my nails in a little pot.

'As soon as I dared to break my Oath, or even thought of doing so, occult powers would turn against me. Even I, a Catholic girl, knew very well that these were no idle words, for the influence of ju-ju pressed heavily on our daily lives...'

Grace returned a second time to the same ju-ju priest for more 'protection'. This time, she was forced to have sex with him while others watched.

A matter of human dignity

While many people are horrified at the brutality of sex trafficking, they prefer to ignore the woman or man prostituting on local street corners. This tendency to focus on whether someone has chosen to engage in prostitution or not is anti-gospel and misses the point, says Mark Wakeling, director of the National Christian Alliance on Prostitution in the UK.[27]

Mark doesn't deny personal choice, but says we need to ask, 'Why do people make those choices in the first place?' The choice to engage in sexual exploitation is faced by vulnerable people whose options are severely limited. Their 'choice' is often one of survival.

'Jesus didn't show compassion to those that "deserved" it and withdraw from those that didn't,' Mark says. 'There's a huge level of exploitation that happens in the majority of prostitution, and whether someone is moved from point A to point B is irrelevant. It's the exploitation that we're in arms about, not the movement.'

Sigma Huda, the UN Special Rapporteur on Trafficking in Persons, says that in the vast majority of places where prostitution is practiced in the world, it's akin to trafficking in its exploitation.[28]

The Palermo Protocol, the UN's definition of trafficking, does not distinguish between voluntary or forced prostitution. Agreed upon by more than 100 countries, the definition includes not only the victim's deception, but the abuse of power, situations of vulnerability, and human rights abuses such as debt bondage, deprivation of liberty and lack of control over one's work. The definition also applies to exploitation within one's own country. Whether the victim of trafficking consented to be exploited is irrelevant.[29]

'Loverboys'

In the Netherlands, Dutch teenagers are groomed by 'loverboys', men who initially pose as boyfriends in order to pimp girls. The men, usually 18 to 25, seek vulnerable girls with broken home lives, learning difficulties or mental problems. The manipulation strategy consists of wooing a 16- to 18-year-old girl with expensive gifts and words of romance, until she has sex with the man and feels blindly in love.

Then he begins enslaving her. He doesn't let her out of his sight, following her wherever she goes. The lover-boy may ask the smitten girl to do a sexual favor for a friend as proof of her love. He often requests that she get tatooed with his name to prove her fidelity and show his ownership over her. Soon, he insists that she prostitute herself, threatening her with beatings or harm to her family. The loverboy watches the girl from the street or bridges in the red-light district to ensure she doesn't escape. The girl is forced to give all her money to him and is frequently threatened.[30]

An estimated 2,000 Dutch girls under the age of 18 work in prostitution. Many Dutch women in prostitution say they started prostituting because of a loverboy, but eventually began working for themselves.[31]

ONE STEP FURTHER

Read: Luke 4:16–20:

He went to Nazareth, where he had been brought up, and on the Sabbath day he went into the synagogue, as was his custom. And he stood up to read. The scroll of the prophet Isaiah was handed to him. Unrolling it, he found the place where it is written: 'The Spirit of the Lord is on me, because he has anointed me to preach good news to the poor. He has sent me to proclaim free-dom for the prisoners and recovery of sight for the blind, to release the oppressed, to proclaim the year of the Lord's favor.'

'Then he rolled up the scroll, gave it back to the attendant and sat down. The eyes of everyone in the synagogue were fastened on him.'

Reflect: How does Jesus describe his mission? Do you think he would see trafficked women differently from prostituted women? Do we? Why is that? Is it right?

Pray: For the release of trafficked and prostituted women around the world. Pray for the men and women who seduce and control them, that God would change their hearts. Ask God how he desires you to share his concern for women and men oppressed and blinded by sexual exploitation.

CHAPTER 6

The Sexualization of American Culture

American culture glorifies unrestrained sex and is normalizing commercial sexual exploitation, says Lisa Thompson, the Salvation Army's Liaison for the Abolition of Sexual Trafficking. Hollywood movies like *Hustle & Flow*, which features the 2006 Oscar-winning song 'It's Hard Out There for a Pimp', and the children's clothing line, 'Pimpfants', contribute to desensitizing society to the brutality of pimping and prostitution. 'We are like frogs in the pot,' Lisa says. 'The water keeps getting hotter and hotter, and we keep sitting there.'[1]

The US is not alone in this malaise of increasing tolerance and demand for sexual exploitation. Worldwide, child pornography and sex tourism have become major industries, facilitated by the expanding Internet, which offers multiple choices to 'consumers' with the ease of clicking a mouse. In the UK, the number of men purchasing sex has doubled in the last decade.[2] An estimated one in four Greek men regularly use women in prostitution.[3]

Levels of demand

Demand for victims of commercial sex can be categorized in three ways, according to Professor Donna Hughes.[4]

The primary factor or level of demand is the men, and occasional women, who seek women, children and sometimes men, for purchasing commercial sex acts. Without these sex buyers, prostitution and sex trafficking would not exist.

The second level is the profiteers – the traffickers, pimps, brothel owners and corrupt officials who profit from supplying victims. These people may participate in transnational organized crime networks.

The third level is the culture that indirectly creates demand for victims by normalizing prostitution and other forms of commercial sex. The media that glamorize things such as stripping, lap dancing and pimping influence public opinion. These images tend to suggest that prostitution is victimless or empowering for women, and may overlook the violence and victimization involved.

This third level of demand is evident in American culture and the rising sexualization of girls and women in the mass media. Sexualization occurs 'when a person's value comes only from his/her sexual appeal or behavior, to the exclusion of other characteristics, and when a person is sexually objectified, e.g., made into a thing for another's sexual use.'[5]

Sexualization in the media

Increasing examples of the sexualization of girls in the media are evident as access to media becomes more omnipresent and 'new media' are created, states an American Psychological Association report on the sexualization of girls. These sexualized images in advertising, merchandising and the media harm women and girls, in addition to having a negative impact on men and boys.[6]

Lisa points to hip-hop kings such as Snoop Dog, who has enjoyed huge popularity and visibility in the mainstream media, despite his pornographic music videos. In 2006, the cover of *Rolling Stone* magazine featured Snoop Dog as 'America's Most Loveable Pimp'. He arrived at the MTV awards three years earlier accompanied by two women on leashes called 'Delicious' and 'Cream'. In the *Rolling Stone* article he says, 'If you really a pimp, you should be able to get two bitches to walk on a leash with you down the red carpet and be yo ho's for the night. And when I did it, it really was pimpin'.'[7] Corporate America further legitimized Snoop Dog when former Chrysler chairman Lee Iacocca appeared in a TV commercial for Chrysler with him.

Snoop Dog and other hip-hop musicians are influencing sexual promiscuity as far away as Amsterdam. Willem Heemskerk, manager of Scarlet Cord, says the hip-hop scene has played a significant role in the disintegration of boundaries surrounding sexuality for Dutch teens.[8] In the ministry's prevention program for high-school girls, a key lesson is focusing on media messages, helping teens understand the lyrics of the music they listen to and grasp the underlying message.

Popular music lyrics that sexualize or degrade women

So blow me bitch I don't rock for cancer/ I rock for the cash and the topless dancers.

Kid Rock, 'f*ck off', 1998

Don'tcha wish your girlfriend was hot like me?

Pussycat Dolls, 2005

That's the way you like to f***... rough sex make it hurt, in the garden all in the dirt.

Ludacris, 2000

I tell the hos all the time, Bitch get in my car.

50 Cent, 2005

Ho shake your ass.   Ying Yang Twins, 2003[9]

The increasing sexualization of women and girls is also evident in American TV shows, Thompson says. Stripping gained more acceptability when Oprah Winfrey, a cultural trendsetter, featured striptease workouts, lap-dancing techniques and pole dancing as a new and freeing form of women's exercise on her TV show in 2003. Since then, spin-off classes to help 'empower' women while they get fit have sprung up around the country.[10]

In 2004, the TV show *The Swan* selected women who were considered society's 'ugly ducklings' and had them undergo massive plastic surgery to become 'swans'. Breast implants have become the most popular form of cosmetic surgery in the nation. Between 2000 and 2006, the number of patients who increased their breast size rose by 55 per cent.[11]

Trends in clothing for girls reflect and promote a rising acceptability of promiscuous behavior. In 2002, the popular clothing store Abercrombie & Fitch promoted thong underwear in children's sizes with the words 'eye-candy' and 'wink-wink' printed on the front.[12] Children's Halloween costumes for pimps and prostitutes are also not unusual.[13]

Bratz, a brand of popular children's dolls in the US, UK, France, Spain and Italy emphasize girls' fashions.[14] The dolls have been criticized by groups such as the American Psychological Association for their *risqué* outfits:

Bratz dolls come dressed in sexualized clothing such as miniskirts, fishnet stockings, and feather boas. Although these dolls may present no more sexualization of girls or women than is seen in MTV videos, it is worrisome when dolls designed specifically for 4- to 8-year-olds are associated with an objectified adult sexuality.[15]

Sexual idolatry

The insidious sexualization of culture is one of Satan's timeless tactics, says Mario Bergner, founder of Redeemed Lives, an international ministry to sexually broken people.[16] 'Satan takes the worship that we're to give to God and turns it into sexual idolatry – a worship of each other's bodies.'

Sexual idolatry has been around for centuries. In Old Testament times, Jewish men and women were tempted to follow Canaanite worship practices that included immoral sexuality. In Paul's first letter to the Corinthian church, he refers to rampant sexual sin in Corinth, the Ancient Near East's hub for commercial sexual exploitation (1 Corinthians 6:11). Worshipers at Corinth's Temple of Aphrodite engaged in sex with temple prostitutes, hoping to ensure a good harvest.

'The enemy seeks to desecrate what he competes with – God and Jesus,' Mario says. 'The image of God on earth is male and female together,' so attacking the image of God in humanity obstructs our worship of the Creator.

Sexualized images of women in the media increase[17]

Music: 84 per cent of music videos on Black Entertainment Television included sexual imagery – most commonly sexual objectification and women dancing sexually (L. M. Ward and Rivadeneyra, 2002).

Video games: 27 per cent of teen-rated video games (in a sample of 80 games of 396 released in 2001) contained sexual themes. Female characters were far more likely than males to be partially nude or engaged in sexual behaviors; 46 per cent of female characters had pronounced cleavage, large breasts, or provocative clothing (Haninger and Thompson, 2004).

Internet porn: 70 per cent of teens 15–17 years of age accidentally encountered pornography on the Internet; 23 per cent said this happened often or very often (Kaiser Family Foundation, 2001).

Magazine ads: In ads from six women's magazines published over twenty years, women shown as suggestively dressed, partially clad or nude increased from 28 per cent in 1983 to 49 per cent in 2003 (Reichert and Carpenter, 2004).

Celebrity ads: In such ads, stars popular with teenagers and pre-teens appear in highly sexualized poses. Some ads play up innocence as sexy, such as a Sketchers' 'Naughty and Nice' shoe ad that featured pop singer Christina Aguilera dressed as a schoolgirl in pigtails, with her shirt unbuttoned, licking a lollipop.

ONE STEP FURTHER

Read: Romans 12:2 says, 'Do not conform any longer to the pattern of this world, but be transformed by the renewing of your mind. Then you will be able to test and approve what God's will is – his good, pleasing and perfect will.'

Reflect: What examples of sexualization in your culture can you think of? How can you challenge these messages of sexuality? Equally important, do you see any opportunities to voice appreciation for positive messages in the media about sexuality? Options may include writing a letter or email to a clothing company, celebrity, TV or radio station, website or magazine.

Pray: That God gives you a mind of discernment in your culture. Ask for courage to voice disagreement about harmful messages about sexuality. Pray and consider how you or your church could offer mentors and role models in your community for girls and boys who need to hear about healthy relationships and sexuality.

CHAPTER 7

Online Porn and Sexual Addictions

Mark Laaser had an unquenchable desire for secret sex. On the outside, he was a respected pastor, counselor, husband and father of three. But he says that wasn't enough to fill the lonely, angry part of himself that considered sex a solution to his needs.[1]

Sex gave him a high that seemed to fill the loneliness inside. 'It was just an excitement, a raw excitement – kind of like what a drug addict would describe,' he says. 'It was just a high.' It started when Mark was only 11 and discovered pornographic pictures. Fixated, he started stealing porn magazines from the local drugstore, although as a pastor's son, he knew stealing was wrong. From there, he started crossing other moral boundaries because the high was so intense.[2]

In high school he met and dated Debbie, the girl he thought would change him. But Mark hid his secret sins from her and everyone else, hoping that married life would fulfill him. They married right after college.[3] Although Mark loved his wife deeply, 'I was amazed early on, even in the first year of marriage, that my temptation to masturbate and look at pornography returned rather quickly,' he says.[4]

Unlike someone who just likes sex, Mark was becoming addicted. 'I wanted to experience it. I wanted to act it out. Eventually I had a lot of preoccupation with planning or doing or thinking what it would be like,' he says.[5]

In college, Mark watched porn videos[6] and masturbated excessively.[7] In seminary and while completing a doctorate in psychology, Mark visited X-rated bookstores and made monthly visits to 'massage parlors' where he paid for sex with so-called 'masseuses', a habit he kept from Debbie and continued into his career as a pastor and counselor.[8]

Even as he pastored and practiced counseling, Mark fed his sexual addiction, although he felt guilty and nervous about being caught. He initiated affairs with multiple female clients over a ten-year period, confusing sex with love and believing he cared for them. He repeatedly vowed to end the affairs, but continued to fall into sin until several colleagues confronted him. One of them, a recovering alcoholic, told him, 'You know, your behaviors with sex seem like mine with alcohol. You're out of control. Why don't you let us find you some help?'[9]

Although afraid, Mark was tired of his double life and began recovery treatment for sexual addiction. He worked through childhood memories, the guilt of his past and anguish over his abuse of others, but also discovered joy in honesty and restored relationships with his wife and friends. Several clients sued him. He never preached from the pulpit again, but found freedom in God's forgiveness, something he never felt he had deserved. Through his healing, Mark discovered a new ministry in helping others recovering from sexual addiction. Today he is an author, speaker and the founder of Faithful and True Ministries, a counseling center for sexual addictions. He says, 'It is because of my own desperation that I reach out to others in theirs.'[10]

Sexual sin is not news for me or you, but understanding it is critical for us as Christians. Shocked and embarrassed at a person's moral failure, we often fail to examine our own sin, shame and fears. Examining what leads to addictive sexual behaviors can enable us to offer Christ's hope to those who have been hurt by others or who have suffered secretly from sexual sin.

Online porn: The Triple A Engine

'Internet porn is the crack cocaine of addiction,' Mark says. Dubbed the 'Triple A Engine', Internet porn has enabled accessible, anonymous and affordable viewing. The Web is *accessible* from the privacy of one's home or office, offers *affordable* or often free porn, and is *anonymous* because users think no one knows what they're doing.[11]

Mark adds a fourth 'A' – *accidental* – due to the porn industry's aggressive attempts to get innocent browsers to stumble across porn sites. In the early nineties the porn industry purchased many domain names for popular people, products or places. For example, one of the Disney character names is a porn site.[12]

'If there was a sexual behavior likely to suck in an otherwise healthy person, it'd be accessing porn on the Internet,' Mark says.[13] The growth of the Web worldwide has made online pornography available to millions of people, generating $2.5 billion in annual revenue in the US alone.[14] Rising numbers of men and women confess to regularly accessing porn on the Internet.

By far the largest sub-set of men who struggle with sexual addiction are dealing specifically with Internet pornography addiction. Worldwide, 72 million people visit adult websites each month, including 40 million American adults who visit online porn sites regularly.[15]

Sadly, the average age of first exposure to online porn is only 11,[16] although Mark has seen cases of 5-year-old children taking their parents' credit cards to access paid online porn.[17] This is not surprising, considering that the average Internet user receives 4.5 pornographic emails per day, and children spend an increasing amount of time on the Web.[18] 'These days kids are incredibly resourceful online,' Mark says. 'Parents need to talk to their children much earlier about sexuality.'[19]

The link between porn and prostitution

The jump between using pornography and engaging prostituted men and women is not far for people struggling with addictive behavior. In a survey of prostituted people in 9 countries, 47 per cent were asked to imitate acts others had seen in pornography, and 49 per cent reported that pornography was made of them.[20]

Porn is also used as a training manual by pimps and traffickers. For example:

> Thirty per cent of the women in one research project reported that their pimps compelled them to imitate scenes from pornography to teach them how to be prostitutes (Giobbe, 1990). One woman, prostituted as a teen and as an adult, said, 'The man who prostituted me showed me pictures of what he was going to do to me and he would "practice" on me what was happening in the picture. That's how I learned what to do for the trick.'[21]

Trafficking victims are also coerced into the production of porn. For example, two girls, aged 12 and 6, sold into prostitution by their relatives, were then sold by a Thai man in Bangkok's Patpong district, famous for its sex venues, to an

Australian man for sex. The two girls were delivered to the tourist's hotel room, where he abused and photographed them for months.[22]

Porn can also play a role in domestic violence. Pornography depicts acts of prostitution, including beatings and rapes of prostituted women. 'Men masturbate to pictures of prostituted women being beaten and raped, and some act out what they see in the porn on their wives and girlfriends.'[23]

Cyber sex is a new form of virtual prostitution in which entrepreneurs in the Internet sex industry are expanding ways to sell flesh online. Strip shows, live sex shows and live Webcams enable consumers to purchase interactive sex shows in the secrecy and privacy of their own homes or offices. High-speed Internet enables traffickers and pimps to exploit victims in their home countries where law and/or law enforcement may be weak.

The Philippines has become one of the world's largest producers of child porn and a center for under-age cyber sex. Children under 18 are paid to perform sex acts in front of Web cameras linked to Internet sites that anyone anywhere in the world can view for a fee.[24]

Operators of child porn and sex trafficking in the Philippines can earn more than $1 billion a year, believes Philippine Senator Maria Ana Consuelo Madrigal. Porn industry producers from wealthier countries are exploiting children from poor families. Some children are sold by their own parents, who don't believe the children are violated because they're not actually being touched while doing lewd acts in front of a camera.[25]

Understanding sexual addiction

The faces behind the demand for commercial sexual exploitation are more familiar than we'd like to think. While it's easy to blame 'those perverts' for victimizing men, women and children, they may also be hurting victims.

The majority of Mark's patients in counseling for sexual addictions have themselves experienced sexual abuse in childhood. Past research indicates that 80 per cent of sex addicts have been sexually abused,[26] although Mark notes that among his patients are people who are simply lonely, isolated, working too much and lacking good relationships. The men he counsels range from doctors to pastors, bankers to trades-people, single and married guys, and all ages.[27]

Sexual addiction is generally, not clinically, defined as any sexual activity that feels out of control. 'A sex addict feels compelled to seek out and engage in sexual behaviour, in spite of the problems it may cause in their personal, social and work lives.'[28] The addiction may include excessive porn use, compulsive masturbation, exhibitionism, voyeurism, fetishes, high-risk sex, prostitution, telephone or Internet sex, multiple affairs and anonymous sexual encounters.

Like drugs and alcohol, sex can be chemically addictive. The body releases powerful neurochemicals during sex that are pleasurable. Some people become addicted to these chemicals and are obsessed with getting their next sexual high. As with other addictions, the body gets used to these chemicals, so the addict needs increasing doses of sex to reach the same buzz.[29]

But after the highs, a person feels the lows – shame, regret, remorse and anxiety. The addict can feel alone and powerless to change his or her behavior. The cycle begins again as he seeks sex as a way to escape the feelings.[30] Gradually, what begins as curiosity can evolve into abuse, dependency and then full-blown addiction.

Eventually, self-identity becomes twisted with the addiction. 'People think, "How could I be so stupid? So foolish? So sinful? So immoral?"' Mark says. 'Addicts generally have a sense that "I'm sinful" but the cycle contributes to their growing sense that "I'm a bad and worthless person."'[31]

As much as 10 per cent of the total Christian population in the US may be sexually addicted, experts speculate.[32] If so, then in a church of 500, as many as 50 men and women may be sex addicts. 'Christians who suffer from this disease have prayed ceaselessly, read the Bible constantly, and consulted with innumerable pastors, but they still can't stop. Discouraged, many leave the church,' Mark writes.[33]

'He [the Devil] uses many dynamics to create sexual addiction, including unhealthy families, abuse, and feelings of shame. The devil convinces us that we are evil people... There is no question in my mind that we are waging warfare with the devil when we attempt to heal sexual addiction.'[34]

The enemy destroys through porn

Mario Bergner, founder of Redeemed Lives, writes:[35]

> The enemy uses porn to destroy our humanity. Porn reduces people to objects in pictures; it depersonalizes us. It destroys the lives of the people in the pictures and those who look at them – both their intimate lives and their sense of self as an intimate being made in the image of God.
>
> The Devil uses porn to establish an idol in the heart. For some men, the cultural acceptance of *Playboy* magazine or soft porn perpetuates an idealized image of women few live up to. If that's his ideal, what he has next to him is not. He becomes less interested in what he does have

because his imagination is held captive by what he doesn't (a pornographic image of a woman). Even worse is when the woman next to him does match the idealized porn image. She is then never seen for the person she is, but only for her external appearance.

In reality, people in the porn industry are deeply wounded. One way to help men break free is to start seeing them as hurting people. I've told men, if you've gone to the same porn sites, start praying for those people and their salvation. There isn't a healthy young man or woman that undresses before a camera – there's always something painful in their souls that led them into the porn industry.

Jill's journey

Men are not the only consumers of pornography. One in six American women (17 per cent) struggles with a porn problem.[36]

Jill* was 6 or 7 years old when a neighbor started abusing her.[37] 'He had porn in front of me while he was abusing me and touching himself. I remember sitting on his lap while he was flipping pages,' she says. Her parents paid little attention to Jill's activities or whereabouts. When she was a teen, another acquaintance molested her in the woods near the family home, porn magazines littered around him.

Jill's parents weren't Christians but they dropped her and her two brothers off at a Baptist church on Sunday mornings. Jill became a Christian in the 5th grade. But she struggled with depression, drinking and suicidal thoughts from her teens into adulthood and saw various counselors. When Jill came to school drunk, as a high-school freshman, she was suspended.

Her mother picked her up from school, then made Jill mow the lawn instead of addressing her drunkenness.

In Jill's twenties, she began renting highly graphic R-rated movies. Then, when the Internet was connected in her home, it became easy to access porn online. Curiosity and boredom were the initial triggers. 'Pornography was my hobby,' she says.

The porn led to a masturbation addiction. Jill still struggles with masturbation, although she's found much healing. The first time she pulled out her credit card to pay for online porn, she was gripped with fear. 'From that point, I actively sought healing. It was going beyond what even I thought was acceptable,' she says. She confessed her problems to a close Christian friend who prayed for her and urged her to seek help.

Jill joined a local ministry called Redeemed Lives that provides biblical counseling and prayer groups for Christians struggling with sexual brokenness and other issues. The healing process hasn't been easy. She knows that the anger she buried for years was a big reason for her addiction. And she understands the cycle of shame she's endured.

'I've been so lonely and I didn't have a lot in my life – that kept it [the addiction] alive,' she says. 'I had down time between 5 p.m. until midnight every day and all week-end. I didn't do anything.'

For the last five years, Jill has tried to fill her life with healthy friendships, church ministry and caring for others. Finding a church that felt safe was also key. Church of the Resurrection (Wheaton, IL) offers one-on-one prayer with trained prayer ministers during every Sunday service. Convicted by the Holy Spirit, Jill decided to confess her masturbation problem to a prayer minister every Sunday for three months. Although she's also seen a counselor off and on for twenty-five years, she says, 'I didn't find healing there, I found it in God.' Besides the counseling, 'confession and staying connected at church' are critical.

Today Jill works at a Christian non-profit organization where she still struggles with the pornographic emails she receives daily in her work account. An extra layer of defensive software helps to provide protection, but some still get through the filter. 'We're bombarded with images,' she says. 'I just have to keep confessing.'

ONE STEP FURTHER

Read: Psalm 119 is the repentant prayer of a sinner, whether confessing a sexual sin or any other type of sin:

> I am laid low in the dust; preserve my life according to your word. I recounted my ways and you answered me; teach me your decrees... My soul is weary with sorrow; strengthen me according to your word. Keep me from deceitful ways; be gracious to me through your law...
>
> Turn my eyes away from worthless things; preserve my life according to your word... Take away the disgrace I dread, for your laws are good... Before I was afflicted I went astray, but now I obey your word... It was good for me to be afflicted so that I might learn your decrees...
>
> I have strayed like a lost sheep. Seek your servant, for I have not forgotten your commands.

Reflect: How do you feel about this plague of sexual addiction in our society? Are you shocked? Can you relate? Like Mark and Jill, we are all sinners in need of God's grace, both generally and in our sexuality.

What attitudes toward sexual brokenness are spoken or unspoken in your home and community? Do our communities provide opportunities for confession and accountability?

Do you maintain accountability to anyone concerning your own computer time and viewing? Your children's?

Pray: Examine your heart for any condemnation toward people who struggle with sexual sin or those who are exploited. Ask for God's forgiveness and a heart of compassion toward them. Pray for changed attitudes and support structures that facilitate healing and freedom in your own community or church.

PART 2

Stories of Hope

CHAPTER 8

Inside Brothels: Birds in a Cage

I talked with Myrto Theocharous at a coffee shop on a snowy Chicago day last winter. She had been a dedicated volunteer for Nea Zoi (Greek for 'Lost Coin'), an International Teams ministry to trafficked and prostituted men and women in Athens, Greece. Now she was a grad student studying theology. She planned to return to Greece and teach in a Bible school or seminary about God's love for women and men on the streets. Here she describes how God called her to reach women in brothels:[1]

In the summer of 2004 Jesus shook me out of my sleep, like a father going crazy for his daughters. Jesus' daughters have been kidnapped. His babies are sitting in bondage and he called me and said to me:

'I want you to go and find my daughters who are sitting in bondage. They are waiting day and night for someone to search them out, someone to go into their dark and dirty brothels and call their name, someone to open the door and let the light in.

'Tell them that their Father loves them. Tell them that they have been deceived and they don't belong there – they should never believe that they belong there. Tell them that I sent you, hug them like I would hug them, kiss them like I would kiss them, clothe them, feed them and caress their hair like I would.

'Look them in the eye and see what I, their Father, see. See their bright futures, see their beautiful lives, see them in their true home where they belong. Do not call them prostitutes because I have a name for them. I created them in my image. They are mine.'

So one night two more girls and I got a little basket and filled it with cookies, warm coffee, tea and hot chocolate, New Testaments and tracts, and we started walking toward their neighborhoods. I was scared. I was afraid I wouldn't see his daughters with the same eyes that he sees them. A small voice inside me was whispering that their appearance may intimidate me, they may shut me out. Maybe they got comfortable tied up in their bondage and they don't want me to go and disturb them. Maybe I will be intruding in their lives, maybe this is their choice and I should respect that. Maybe, maybe, maybe…

But then I hear their Father's voice crying out: 'No! These are lies! My children don't belong there, they are mine. No! They may seem comfortable there but that's because they are blind, they are numb, they are in chains. Go get my daughters.'

Several months after talking with Myrto, I traveled to Athens for a week to visit Nea Zoi and discover first-hand God's heart for his sons and daughters in prostitution. It's a Monday night, and I'm sitting in the small, third-floor office of Nea Zoi with staff and about eight other volunteers.

'Sometimes volunteers want to grab girls, hug them and say, "God loves you; now change!"' Eirini Chatzigiani, a young Greek social worker, tells us. She is orienting us, the new volunteers who will visit the brothels that spring night.[2]

'Our approach is to offer a relationship, earn their trust, answer their needs, be human and show them the Lord, not just speak about God,' she says.

'We never go alone, always in groups of more than two. A guy always comes and stands outside and prays that the Lord guides us and our conversation,' she says. The guy also serves as protection.

My adrenaline is pumping with the thrill of joining others who are shining Christ's light in the devil's bedrooms. The cautions in the volunteer orientation manual offer helpful perspective:

> Consider telling someone that 'God loves you' when she defines the words this way:
>
> *God:* Creator of this messed up world, the one who has the power to make my life better but for some reason does not.
>
> *Love:* Sex, anything other than active violence.
>
> *Self:* Failure, stupid, a jinxed thing. Something unlovable.
>
> What might she hear if she defines 'God loves you' in this way? Maybe something similar to… Mandarin Chinese. Or worse, maybe this person would recall all of her negative experiences with Christians and think, 'Uh oh, these people are Christians – I'd better not let them know how screwed up I am.'[3]

Sharing the gospel with women and men in prostitution takes place within the context of relationships. Although their cultures, ethnicities, family backgrounds and specific circumstances differ, 'all struggle with shame and feelings of abandonment by God, anger, and worthlessness.'[4]

Prostitution in Greece

Prostitution is legal in Greece, but only by permit within a licensed brothel. Women who want a prostitution permit must also have a valid work permit, be free of disease and unmarried. They must also get weekly health checks at the Department of Health.[5]

Since licenses for brothels are hard to obtain, of some 300 brothels in downtown Athens, only a tiny minority are legal. Even among the few licensed brothels, women may work in them illegally. Brothels run twenty-four hours a day, with one woman working a six-to-eight-hour solo shift in each. Some women work two shifts back-to-back. The average price is 20 Euros per client. Besides the prostituted woman, a man or woman working as pimp or madam usually takes a shift and greets customers, getting a cut of the pay.

After thirty minutes of singing praise songs and praying, my team walks a few blocks to Iasonos, a street lined with decaying buildings serving as cheap brothels. The lights lit above a doorway indicate a brothel is open for business. These brothels are staffed by mostly Greek and Eastern European women. We stop in front of one where Nea Zoi teams have been welcomed before. I wait outside, praying that the two Nea Zoi women are allowed inside the brothel and are not distracted by any customers. That night, our team only has time to visit three or four brothels. Each time, the women inside are eager for conversation. I never have a chance to go in because our time runs out.

We head back to the office for debriefing. Eirini tells us that they spent thirty minutes talking at the first brothel, and the woman begged them to stay longer.

That night Maria, a prostituted Albanian woman, was so eager to talk with the Lost Coin pair that she kept six or seven men waiting for her. When Maria had learned she was pregnant back in Albania, her boyfriend had advised her to abort the baby. She and her parents had refused. Now a single mother, Maria supported her five-year-old son who lived with her parents back in Albania. A recent visit home had been unbearable for her. Her son didn't want to call her 'Mom'. Depressed, she lost her appetite and was only eating several spoonfuls a day. Her weight dropped to 48 kilograms. Before the Nea Zoi pair left, she asked them to visit her friend, Anna, in another brothel on Wednesday.

Another Greek volunteer speaks up: 'We prayed God would open doors, that there wouldn't be obstacles. There were men who came in and went out of the brothel while we were there, but none bothered us. God heard our prayers.'

Some women in the brothels welcome conversation that helps pass the long monotonous nights, but few accept offers for help finding another job or shelter. 'It's like birds in a cage. You open the door, but they don't fly out,' Myrto had told me back in Chicago-land. 'They don't take this opportunity because they don't have a concept of a person who just wants to give and get nothing in return. They've never had this in their life. It's suspicious to them. It takes a long time for them to consider your offer.'[6]

Low self-esteem is one of the chains that keep women in brothels. 'These women can be set free, but they don't think they deserve it. They've grown up learning what love is through sexual abuse or rape,' Myrto said.[7]

Christians have been praying over Iasonos for eight years. Over time, their prayer and perseverance have opened doors.

The battle between kingdoms

The ministry is small and committed volunteers are few in number. 'At night it's cold downtown in the city, in the filthiest possible place. There are murders there. Nobody wants to go,' Myrto said. Each time Myrto planned to volunteer, a million excuses would arise in her head. Gradually she realized it was the enemy's opposition. To cope, she and another volunteer agreed to call and remind each other: 'Hey, the devil will probably give you a lot of excuses for not going, but we need to go.'[8]

'We really had to push each other,' Myrto told me. But the opposition is both a calling and a testing, she believes. 'When you have a calling, you have to live it out on a daily basis – it's a decision to live by that calling. I think of Abraham who was called to be the father of a great nation, but he was tested every step of the way.'

Myrto gradually realized that the battle in the brothel is the Lord's, although she must be prepared for it. Once Myrto and another woman entered a brothel while two male volunteers waited outside and prayed. 'We wanted to speak to the girl who worked there. But the pimp wouldn't let us talk to her – he kept chatting very loudly, trying to distract our attention. We recognized this was from the devil. "Why doesn't God shut his mouth?"' we wondered.

'The other volunteer started talking to the girl while I kept talking to him. All of a sudden, he calmed down and I talked with him about his life. The volunteer prayed with the girl and shared the gospel, while tears ran down the girl's face. It's like he [the pimp] was blinded to what was going on. The room was only about ten feet by four. The volunteer and the girl talked, prayed and exchanged phone numbers.'

Back outside, the two guys said, 'We were praying and God told us to pray, "Shut his mouth."' They had no idea what was transpiring in the brothel.

'That was confirmation it was God's doing. It's his work. He takes care of it and puts the prayers in our mouths,' Myrto says.[9]

Prince Charming

One sunny Wednesday morning, I head back to the Nea Zoi office for another outreach. This time we're headed for Fylis, a residential neighborhood where decrepit apartment buildings stand side-by-side with brothels. The streets are crowded with construction workers, women pushing strollers, and the occasional 'customer' cruising up to a brothel doorway on his motorbike. With our wicker baskets and thermoses, we attract more attention in the bright sunlight from passers-by.

Nea Zoi teams have only been visiting this neighborhood weekly for six months, so they don't have as many friendships and the hostility is palpable. Door after door is closed in our faces.

'We're eating door,' Eirini says. That's a literal translation for the Greek equivalent of 'We got the door slammed in our face,' she tells me.

We learn at one brothel that all the brothels on that street are closing temporarily. Someone has tipped them off that the police are planning a raid, and word has spread quickly.

We walk down several more blocks to another street. At a brothel where Emma has had friendly talks with the Greek woman who works as a madam, I enter cautiously with her. We pass through a gate, then down a sidewalk to an enclosed and crumbling tile stairway. We climb the steps, reach the door, and knock. An older woman with graying hair motions us in, smiling. The waiting room is dim and smoky, lit faintly with red Christmas lights. I barely make out a couple of benches lining the wall. Pop music blares.

We follow the woman into a brightly lit room where the news is playing on a small TV. A young woman with a tinted red bob and startling green eyes stands up and shakes our hands, introducing herself as Tonya.* Emma tells me that Tonya is from Russia. I look Tonya in the eyes and try to avoid staring at her racy black lingerie and plunging neckline. The older woman, Athena,* pulls in a few chairs for us.

Emma offers tea, which they decline, and tells them that I'm visiting from Chicago. That grabs Tonya's interest. 'I'm dating a Greek-American from Washington, DC,' she says in Greek, while Emma translates for me. 'I'm going to marry him.'

'Yes, she's going to stop this job in six months,' Athena affirms in English.

'Congratulations! When are you getting married?' I ask.

'Well, there's no wedding date yet,' Tonya replies. She says that first she must visit DC and see how she likes it.

'He's a real gentleman,' Athena says.

During the conversation, I take in my surroundings. The room contains a large dressing-table and mirror. Condoms wrapped in plastic are laying on the dressing-table. On the walls, Greek icons of various saints stare at us. A tall window lets in daylight from the courtyard.

We hear a bell and Tonya excuses herself. We chat with Athena about her family for a few minutes before Tonya returns. Evidently, a potential customer decided to 'shop' else-where. We leave when Athena thanks us for coming.

Tonya's 'Prince Charming' may only be a regular customer who flatters her with hollow promises – this is not unusual, Emma says. We pray she places her trust in the Father who will never betray her.

I ask about the Greek icons later. 'We Greeks are Orthodox, so they believe in the saints. They have an icon to protect them. They're religious people,' explains Dina, a Greek volunteer. The Greek women she meets are interested in hearing about church. The Eastern Europeans tend to be atheist or Orthodox, but have heard little religious teaching.[10]

Called outside the church

Dina Petrou, age 45, is a regular volunteer. She learned about Nea Zoi when a staff member spoke at her church. Every Wednesday she visits brothels with Nea Zoi in the Fylis area of downtown Athens.[11]

'Most Greeks, even in the church, feel these are dirty women,' Dina says. 'Some Christians feel we're not supposed to be there [in the red-light district].' The first time Dina volunteered she was nervous, but since then she's become comfortable, she tells me. 'I feel called to reach people outside the church.'

In one brothel, Dina has become friends with a woman working as a madam. Tina* had a good job in a bank and two university degrees. But when her husband fell ill, the couple moved from Cyprus to Greece for better medical care. The hospital fees proved expensive, so to cover the costs, Tina took the brothel job. She keeps her work a secret from her husband, who remains in a private hospital. She gets a cut of 5 Euros per customer. 'I'm praying to stop this work,' she told Dina, and asked for prayer.

Dina is thankful for her husband's and children's support. 'My family prays for me,' she says. 'My 10-year-old son and I are praying for another woman in a brothel who came to the Second Evangelical Church years ago.'

Dina is also raising awareness about the ministry among her friends, at her son's elementary school, and in church. 'I'm praying that I'll be an example for them and my kids,' she says.

ONE STEP FURTHER

Read: Joshua 2, where God's people encounter Rahab. Then read Matthew 1:5.

Reflect: Jesus' ancestor, Rahab, is the first recorded prostituted woman in Scripture who confesses belief in the Lord. 'I know that the LORD has given this land to you and... the LORD your God is God in heaven above and on the earth below,' she tells the Jewish spies sent to scope out the Promised Land.

The story of Rahab illustrates God's desire to redeem the lowly and stigmatized of society. Nobody is too broken for God to save or use in accomplishing his purposes. We are all unworthy of God's grace and equally in need of Jesus' saving power.

Pray: For God to send more witnesses to his sons and daughters in chains. Jesus is waiting to introduce us to the people he loves. Pray their eyes would be opened to their true identity as God's beloved children.

Amsterdam

The Cleft, a YWAM ministry, located in Amsterdam's central red-light district since 1979, shares the gospel with people struggling with prostitution, homelessness and drug addictions. Photo by the author

Red neon lights hang above windows just past the Scarlet Cord's humble entrance in Amsterdam. Jesus' followers are located in the center of the devil's bedroom. Photo by the author

Brazil

Roberto was prostituting himself as a transvestite in São Paolo's infamous Luz neighborhood to earn cash for his next crack smoke. 'Instead of transvestites and drug dealers, God prepared a new place for me,' Roberto told me. – São Paulo, Brazil. Photo by Patrícia Croitor Evangelista

A four-month stint in the squalor of a São Paulo jail pushed Roberto to choose between heaven and hell. 'I saw hell in prison – fighting, drugs and prostitution,' he says. Desperate, one day he cried out to God, 'What do you want me to do?'
Photo by Patrícia Croitor Evangelista

'I pray that the other transvestites look at me and see that God can change them also.' – Roberto, São Paulo, Brazil

Emmaus

Prostituted men in Chicago find hot showers, laundry facilities, homecooked meals, Bible studies, and people like founder John Green (2nd from right) of Emmaus Ministries, who care whether they live or die.

Photo by Michael Hudson

The basement chapel of Emmaus Ministries' drop-in center. About forty men enjoy reprieve from the streets each month where dinner is served family style.

Photo by Michael Hudson

'If we see a guy on the street, and he's filthy or he smells bad, and he comes up and wants a hug, I'm gonna hug him,' says Sil Davis of Emmaus Ministries, Chicago.

Photo by Michael Hudson

Harmony Dust

Harmony Dust danced four nights a week at a strip-club near the L.A. airport during college. 'I was so unhappy. The pain was suffocating,' she said.

Photo by Emily Hibard

After finding freedom in Christ and healing from sexual abuse, Harmony married a godly man, John Dust, whom she met at her church.
Photo by Emily Hibard

Once a month, Harmony and a dozen or so young Christian women pile into a van and head to 10 to 12 seedy night clubs in L.A.
Photo by Emily Hibard

India – Freeset

Today, more than 100 former prostituting women in Kolkata, India, work from 10 a.m. to 7 p.m. at Freeset, sewing 150,000 jute tote and gift bags a year.

Photo by Kerry Hilton, Freeset

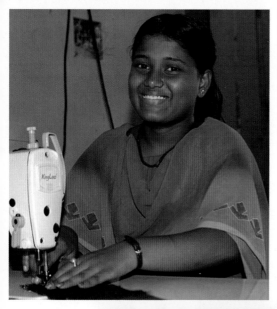

Women pray daily at Freeset and meet in prayer cells each Wednesday. Local pastors frequently lead devotions. The women return home to the same place where they used to serve customers.
Photo by Kerry Hilton, Freeset

'We're seeking a business takeover – a freedom business takeover of the sex business.' – Kerry Hilton, Freeset
Photo by Kerry Hilton, Freeset

Nea Zoi – Athens

A 'customer's' motorbike stands outside a brothel door in downtown Athens. The lit bulb over the doorway indicates that the brothel is open.

Photo by the author

A sunny Wednesday morning. Volunteers and staff from Nea Zoi tote carafes of hot tea and baskets filled with literature and cookies to brothels in Athens.

Photo by the author

Rahab Fdn Jamelyn

After-school activities for teen girls at risk or involved in prostitution help boost their self-esteem and trust in God. – Rahab Foundation, San José, Costa Rica.
Photo by Jamelyn Lederhouse

Samaritana

Bevs (left) and I outside the garden chapel at Samaritana. 'I realized that aside from being saved from prostitution, I also became an instrument for my family and other people to know about God,' Bevs says. – Manila, Philippines.
Photo by the author

Thelma Nambu (left) of Samaritana helps women like Bevs discover they are created in the image of God by respecting them, affirming their sadness, and 'diving for the deepest pearl in their lives' – signs of a person's true identity. – Manila, Philippines. Photo by the author

Women at Samaritana share chores such as cooking and cleaning.
– Manila, Philippines. Photo by the author

Emotional healing and spiritual growth are not isolated to participation in Bible study or counseling, but integrated into daily life as the women read Scripture together, pray, sing, cook, clean, learn handicrafts, and talk in group and one-on-one counseling sessions. Photo by the author

Thailand

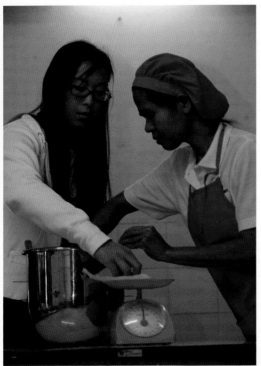

Brittney Quinn (left) of Just Food, Inc., bakes cookies with Joy, who left a life of prostitution and now cooks at a local restaurant.
Photo by International Mission Board

Rachel Thiesen (right), a volunteer with Just Food, Inc., chats with Apple, a prostituting woman and manager of a bar in Chiang Mai, Thailand. Apple and other women look forward to twice-weekly visits with volunteers who care about them.
Photo by International Mission Board

Christa Crawford (left), of Just Food, Inc., with Moon, who was sold into prostitution at age 13. Moon, with her knowledge of human trafficking, helps train staff to work with exploited street kids and victims of trafficking.

Photo by International Mission Board

To help former prostituted women learn about Jesus' love for them, volunteers, such as this Thai woman, teach them how to study the Bible and pray.

Photo by International Mission Board

CHAPTER 9

Trafficked Nigerian Women on the Street

During my visit to Nea Zoi, I trekked around downtown Athens with staff and volunteers, learning how they seek and build relationships with men and women on the streets. Trafficked women are the most elusive, changing locations frequently to avoid the authorities.

It's Thursday night after 11 p.m. in downtown Athens. Ten young and scantily dressed Nigerian women are strutting in front of a cheap hotel. Men of all ages are packed in cars cruising slowly by. Some leer, only intending to 'window shop'. When a car stops at the curb, one of the women darts to the driver's side, provocatively hanging her head and bosom through the window. Across the street, a cluster of African men, possibly involved in pimping or trafficking, observe the flesh trade.

The stench of urine is nearly intolerable. Tasos, a male Greek volunteer, and I stand across the street, praying aloud with eyes wide open for God to intervene in this scene. Three women from the Nea Zoi ministry approach the idle Nigerian women toting baskets of Bibles, books, fliers on health and legal rights, cookies and thermoses of hot tea.

97

Suddenly two police officers on motorbikes roar by. The women scatter and flee inside the hotel. The police often intimidate with random passings. There is a real threat of jail-time to those without legal residence or work permits. Unfortunately, they also disrupt our volunteers' precious few minutes of conversation with the women.

Down the block, I watch a similar scene replay only thirty minutes later. But this time, a Nea Zoi leader holds hands with and prays with a statuesque Nigerian woman who has asked for prayer. On the next street are more women and customers in cars in front of another hotel. I watch as one woman pulls down her miniskirt to reveal her derriere as a man decides how much he's willing to pay to use her body.

Rosa* and I offer tea to 'Lisa'*, a petite Nigerian woman with long brown and blonde braids. When she says she likes music, we sing, acappella, a verse we've just sung before hitting the streets: 'He carried the burden of the world on His shoulders… He can carry you, too, my sister.' Then Lisa sings us a verse of an African worship song in a lovely soprano.

Lisa was assistant choir director for her church back in Nigeria and wrote many worship songs herself. But that was before she was trafficked to Greece, lured with the promise of a high-paying job working in an Athens bar. When the meager income failed to cover her living expenses, Lisa's trafficker pulled her into prostitution – a common ploy. She owes 50,000 Euros to him and lives a life of virtual slavery, forbidden to leave her boss's sight except to work the streets at night.

'By the grace of God, one day I'll stop this job,' Lisa tells us.

'It's not your fault you were trafficked. It's a sin that your trafficker committed,' Rosa says. 'You know, you can tell the authorities what he has done and become free, a legal resident here.'

'No, I cannot. My boss knows my family in Nigeria,' she says. Undoubtedly, he has threatened to harm them. 'The girl before me paid a lot of money to someone, now another girl pays her. One day I'll stop this job and then a new girl will pay me all her money.'

My head spins. The trafficking cycle spirals into deeper darkness than I imagined. Lisa's eyes are blinded to the evil of her own enslavement and that of her willingness to traffic another Nigerian woman for the sake of profit.

I sniff the scents of fear, lust and greed mingling among the urine stench rising from these sidewalks. The devil's bedroom is a complex web of lies that traps many victims.

Divine connections

Normally, teams from Nea Zoi have only moments to offer a cup of tea and a few words before a trafficked woman is distracted by a customer, the police or something else. 'You have just a couple of seconds to find an opening,' Jennifer Roemhildt, founder of Nea Zoi, tells me the next morning at the office.[1] A typical conversation is: 'How are you doing?' 'Fine, fine.'

The night I observed was extraordinary. Many women requested Bibles, books or prayer, or just wanted to talk. Intercessory prayer is key to providing critical moments that crack the door open further to friendships and planting seeds of hope.

Before hitting the streets, male and female volunteers and staff always gather in the tiny third-floor reception room of Nea Zoi for thirty minutes to an hour in worship and prayer. They realize their ministry is set on the front lines of a battle for souls, in non-neutral, non-friendly territory. As the Nea Zoi *Orientation Manual* says:

Only the Almighty God has enough strength, compassion, love and grace for the needs we'll meet, even for just one of the individuals we'll talk to. It is as we focus on him and his eternal attributes that we find the resources to reach out… It is as we focus on his beauty that we can look at the evil and ugliness of prostitution without becoming jaded and cynical… In prayer we also acknowledge that the problems faced by the women demand a spiritual solution, and so we intercede on their behalf.[2]

Trafficking in Greece

An estimated 17,000 trafficking victims reside in Greece. Women and children were purchased for commercial sex about 145 million times by some 1.7 million men between 1990 and 2000. Revenue earned by trafficking in Greece was an estimated 6 billion Euros during this decade.[3]

The largest groups of women trafficked into Greece are from Nigeria, the Balkans and the former Soviet Union. A small minority work in licensed brothels, while the majority work elsewhere – on the streets and in hotels, unlicensed brothels, bars, strip-clubs and private apartments. These women range from 18 to 30 years old.[4]

Although prostitution is condoned in Greek society – an estimated one in four Greek men regularly pay for sex[5] – the prostituted person is blamed and criticized. 'Trafficked women are particularly marginalized as foreigners: isolated from the social network of their home country, ignorant of the language, and vulnerable to deportation', says the Nea Zoi manual.[6]

The local Nigerian community also stigmatizes the trafficked women, although it welcomes their business. 'Nobody wants to associate with them unless they buy things from your shop,' says Mary,* a Nigerian cultural mediator at Nea Zoi.[7]

A link to the normal world

By repeatedly visiting the women on their street territory, volunteers seek to establish friendships and offer hope where their lives would not normally intersect. Trusting friendships often take months or even years to develop until a person may accept an invitation to meet at a coffee shop or visit the Nea Zoi office. Beyond visits on the streets, staff and volunteers call women, meet them in cafes, accompany them to medical visits or visit them in detention centers.

'What we have to offer is God in us… People begin to see we genuinely care for them. The next step is to wonder if God cares for them,' Jennifer tells me. Nea Zoi hopes to help people move from 'denial of their problems and despair, to hope for change and a new life, based on God's power and love.'[8]

The informal relationships become a link to the normal world for those trapped in prostitution. The manual says: 'Through these faithful relationships, the women and men have an opportunity to let down their masks – to trust, tell their stories, and become more open with us.'[9]

For women who are trafficked, choosing to leave is complex and risky. 'It's such a huge leap for women to find God trustworthy enough to leave everything when everyone else in their life has betrayed them,' Jennifer says.

The psychological imprisonment of a trafficking victim makes it hard to escape. The manual explains: 'Because a trafficked woman has lost control of her life, it is essential to respect her wishes for her own life and to allow her to initiate these steps. She needs to be the one responsible for her safety and our role is to empower her and give her back control over her own life.'[10]

In addition, Nigerian women face intense pressure to return to Nigeria as a financial success. 'If they return with money, they are the pride of the community, regardless of how they acquired the wealth (although it won't be talked about). If, however, they are deported without money, they are dirty and despoiled, possibly ineligible for marriage.'[11] This cultural pressure undoubtedly weighs heavily on those who wish to leave prostitution.

'Even if I could kidnap the girls on the streets tonight, give them food, clothing, Greek lessons, computer classes, and more, they'd go back on the streets again,' says Emma Skjonsby Manousaridou, director of Nea Zoi. She cites another non-profit organization that rescued trafficked women a few years ago, but the women repeatedly returned to the streets.[12]

'They saw all this money going through their hands. It's really addictive. Their hearts have to change,' Emma tells me. Although the Nigerian women were deceived by lies about a glamorous life in the West and are suffering immensely, at some point they have a responsibility, she says. 'An organization can't come in and take over their lives.'

UK: A Faith-Based Response to Trafficking

After a trafficking survivor escapes or is rescued, a place of refuge is a critical next step for debriefing and processing the trauma she has experienced. 'Only when a person is in a place away from the trauma, abuse, grievous bodily harm, and monetarily sanitized rape, can she start to consider her future and regain a degree of power over her derailed life,' says Dr. Carrie Pemberton, CEO of Churches Alert to Sex Trafficking Across Europe (CHASTE).

In the UK, an ecumenical effort funds nearly one-third of safe housing for trafficking survivors via CHASTE's networking with the Salvation Army and the Medaille Trust, a Catholic charity.

CHASTE has been raising grassroots awareness of trafficking among UK churches through the Not for

Sale campaign, Sthe third week of May. Congregations have the opportunity to recognize the plight of trafficked women across the globe and commit to practical action through legislation, informed prayer and changed behavior.

CHASTE is also lobbying government to improve legislation dealing with demand for prostitution and sex trafficking.

Wanted: Jobs

Mary helps find alternate employment for the Nigerian women or facilitate their return home, if they wish. But jobs are hard to find in Greece's weak socialist economy, and the women's expectations are high. No one wants to return to Nigeria.

Mary helps support her own family by cleaning houses part-time. She found a cleaning job for one woman who wanted to quit prostitution, but after checking out the house, the woman declined the offer. She told Mary, 'It's a cleaning job, the pay is very low and the place is very dirty.'

Although many Nigerian women are interested in starting their own businesses, European labor laws make that a challenge. A recent law passed in Greece stipulates that anyone wanting a business license must first have at least 60,000 Euros in a Greek bank account. The sum is prohibitive for most immigrants.[13]

Mary tries to encourage the women with this advice: 'You don't start from the top down. You start at the bottom and God will promote you,' but she thinks her words fall on deaf ears. 'They have a mind-set of what income they should make,' she says. A woman may earn 30 Euros from sex with one man, but she's been told she can make 1,000 Euros nightly, and she doesn't easily let go of that hope.'

'Even when the girls try to change, they keep going back to prostitution,' Mary says. 'We're treading in the enemy's camp… It takes a higher power to break the bondage.'

Although many of the Nigerian women were Pentecostal churchgoers back home, their understanding of God's power is clouded. One woman told Mary that every night after work, she prayed for God's forgiveness, 'because you can't serve two masters [God and money] at the same time.'

In one brothel, volunteers offered tea to a Nigerian woman who was reading her Bible. 'No thank you, I'm fasting,' she said.

'What are you going to say as a Christian when they have all this in their head, but they still do what they do?' Mary says.

Why Nigeria?

- Levels of corruption and organized crime in Nigeria surpass most other African countries. Many Nigerians have become disillusioned and sought asylum in Europe.[14]
- Trafficking in women is strongly concentrated in Edo state in the south-central part of Nigeria.[15]
- One in three women in Benin City, Edo's capital, admitted in a survey that she had received offers to go to Europe.[16]
- The success of many female emigrants who went to Europe is highly visible in Edo state – for example, in the form of grand houses built with remittances. Working abroad is often viewed as the best strategy for escaping poverty and ensuring a better future for one's family.[17]

- Nigerian women typically come from large polygamous families. They are intensely loyal to their mother, and feel obligated to help provide financially for the other children of their mother. Some women are engaged to someone in Nigeria and expect to return home and marry.[18]

ONE STEP FURTHER

Read: Luke 19:1–9, Jesus meets Zacchaeus.

Reflect: Jesus went out of his way to welcome Zacchaeus into the kingdom, although as a chief tax collector he was one of society's oppressors.

How do you feel about Lisa's plan to begin trafficking other young women? How do you feel about God's love for victimizers as well as victims?

Pray: For the men and women who are abusing and exploiting others sexually. Ask God to change their hearts and bring to them people who will share the good news of Jesus.

CHAPTER 10

Into Strip-clubs:
Treasures Out of Darkness

Today Harmony, age 31, is the founder and director of Treasures, an LA ministry that reaches women in the sex industry. Once a month, Harmony and a dozen or so young Christian women pile into a van and head to several seedy night-clubs in the sprawling city. They come armed with gifts to offer the dancers inside: bags of treats like lip-gloss and jewelry with brochures that tell Harmony's story of meeting God while in the stripping industry. Harmony's story is continued here from Chapter 2.

When Harmony was 21, she took a ballet class at Santa Monica College, where she became friends with Tanya, a young Christian woman with a sparkling personality. Although she initially lied when Tanya asked about her job, the next week Harmony decided to be honest. Tanya's reaction stunned her: 'She didn't judge me... She blew every preconceived notion of what I thought Christians were, out of the water.'[1]

Harmony had little exposure to church or Christians, but she knew she was headed for hell and believed that if God existed, he wouldn't like her. Although she wanted to go to church someday, she believed, 'I don't measure up, I don't fit that bill, I'm not good enough.'

So when Tanya continued talking to Harmony, she was floored. 'I really appreciated that our friendship wasn't hinged on whether I went to church, and didn't have an agenda like, "I'm gonna get another saved for Jesus."'[2]

Tanya invited Harmony to her church, Oasis Christian Center. When Harmony finally visited for a special event and took her first step inside of a church, she loved it. She quickly became a regular at Oasis on Sundays, then on Mondays and Wednesdays for Bible studies. 'There was a lot of instability in my life and I was looking for a home, an anchor,' she said.[3]

Six months later Harmony was still going to Oasis and dancing at the Century Lounge. On Wednesday nights, she'd go to church, then head straight to work. But, 'I began to understand my value and purpose,' she said. And Tanya allowed time for the Holy Spirit to work. 'She never said, "Now that you're going to church, you gotta change,"' Harmony told me.

One night Harmony went to work and felt naked for the first time. When the song 'Purple Rain' came on, she realized she'd been dancing three years. 'I felt as if God had for the first time lifted the blinders off. I knew God was asking me to leave, but in my heart I was saying, "How am I going to pay my bills?" I heard him say, "I'm never gonna let you down; I'm gonna take care of you."' That night she told her manager she was quitting, then she went to her dressing-room and sold all her stage clothes.

Harmony pursued healing through Bible studies, small groups, reading, Christian counseling and a support group for women who'd been sexually abused. She also severed ties with her boyfriend. Eventually she married a godly man from Oasis and graduated from UCLA with a Masters in Social Work. She began using her talent in dancing at church on the dance worship team.

With encouragement from Tanya and her church leadership, Harmony followed a dream to reach women still trapped in the sex industry and headed back to the Century Lounge in 2004. Now, once a month she leads groups of young Christian women to clubs across LA, visiting up to 150 each year. At each club, they distribute gift bags and messages that testify to God's power to create 'treasures out of darkness' (Isaiah 45:3).

On the day of outreach, the women fast and pray. Between ten and fifteen women pile into a large shuttle van and park out of view of the bouncers and doormen. Groups of three women visit each club at a time.[4]

The outreach is focused on building relationships, even with doormen, bouncers, managers and club owners, who can grant or deny access to the club. If they say no on one visit, they may change their mind the next time. 'We approach every person we meet… as if we have a God appointment with them and they are expecting us. We do not go timidly or apologetically,' states the Training Manual.[5]

The Treasures team leaves gift-bags with the doormen or managers if they agree to give the gifts to the women. If they do get access into the club, conversation with the women working inside is simple and respectful of their time and space. It may entail handing a woman a gift and saying, 'Here's a gift for you.' If she wants to talk, she will.[6]

A typical first conversation might be:

'Here you go. This is a gift for you.'

'Really? Why?'

'Just to let you know that you are loved.'

'Who are you?'

'We are a support group for women. Some of us have been in the business ourselves. Our contact information is in the bag if you ever want to contact us confidentially.'[7]

Some women may want to talk right away. Others may be skeptical and prefer to open the gift and brochure in the privacy of their homes.

Treasures receives phone calls and emails from hundreds of women who want to leave the commercial sex industry. Often, they're nervous and hesitant to trust anyone, perhaps because they feel ashamed, Harmony says. 'Sometimes I think when girls contact us they think, "I gotta be ready to quit."'[8]

Anonymity is important for them – for example, in filling out the contact feedback form on the Treasures website with only a name and address. Women have shown up at Harmony's church after receiving the Treasures brochure or a gift-bag, but she doesn't find out until later. In the first half of 2007, sixty women sent in their addresses and received care packages, including Bibles. Ninety women receive Treasures' devotionals and messages of encouragement via email.[9]

Most women contact Treasures and reveal their identities after they leave the sex industry. Harmony, volunteers and staff offer support and a listening ear, but often they refer women to other groups for sexual or physical abuse, a suicide crisis hotline, and a local church. They often accompany women to their first drug or alcohol counseling session, or help them create résumés and offer job referrals.[10]

Above all, they never condemn the women. 'Do you think God is mad at me for dancing?' asked one woman.[11] Harmony reassured her that nothing could separate her from God's love, and that God would make known his plans for her life if she asked.[12]

'Light' by Harmony Dust

I can still picture the way my hands and legs looked under those lights at the strip-club: Creamy and tan, smooth, flawless… without blemish. There is something about the combination of red and black that creates this appealing illusion. They work together to produce some kind of magic that erases wrinkles and dimples, natural companions of any natural woman.

Back in one of those moments, I can see it. There are eyes all over the room. They are looking at me, taking from me. But, if I let the lights hit my eyes just right, I can't see their faces – they too are washed away. I can pretend that I am as alone and isolated as I feel. Everything is dark, though it doesn't seem that way because the lights are in my eyes, blinding me.

Flash forward a few months later to another moment. I feel the water rush out of my hair and my light blue dress: Dunk, lift, whoosh. So much washed away; all of the things I never wanted to be. Though I can't see Him, I know. He is looking at me. I can feel Him near. Brand new in His eyes, I am spotless and without wrinkle. There are no illusions here – just truth. The water slows to a trickle. I can see their faces. I am not alone. I am in the light, fully present. Awake and alive, I rise.

Ellen, 44, is a former schoolteacher and a home-schooling mom in Texas. A friend introduced us via email. For the last five years, Ellen has been visiting local strip-clubs with teams of women who hope to reach the women inside for Jesus. They tote bags of homemade cookies to offer as gifts to the bouncers, managers and women.[13]

Ellen noticed that many women who dance in the clubs sport tatoos. As she made small talk with them in the dressing-rooms, she realized that the tatoos could open doors to talking about Christ. Although Ellen already had a small cherub tatooed to her upper back, she wanted one with a clear message about how Jesus had changed her life.

After praying for a year, Ellen was ready for the second tatoo. On her lower back, a flowery script spells 'Forgiven'.

She couldn't wait to approach a dancer and tell her, 'I like your tatoo. Let me show you mine.'

But the next time Ellen visited a club, she nearly forgot about her tatoo. When she finally remembered and showed it to one girl, 'she got this really blank look on her face, like, "What does that mean?" Well, I thought it was a blank look, but she was blown away.

'That girl called me weeks later and said, "That tatoo on your back was a sign, because I was raised in the church and I know what that means." That same girl stopped dancing in the strip-club.'

Chances of sharing the gospel in a strip-club are slim, Ellen says. Volunteers have other worries: 'What are you gonna do when a naked girl comes to hug you? Are you gonna stiffen up or jump back? We give lots of hugs. What are you gonna do if one comes onto you – there's a lot of lesbian stuff going on. My comment was, "No thank you, I'm married."

'What do you do when a girl is so drunk she's falling all over the floor? You pick her up off the floor and help her dress so she can leave. You don't make comments behind people's backs. You don't gasp because there are cameras all over the place.'

Ellen is quick to note that not everyone is ready for outreach. On a recent visit to a large strip-club, three first-time volunteers were shaken by the giant posters of naked women in compromising poses with other women. To avoid the obvious evil present, Ellen focuses her eyes elsewhere. 'You need to go in there prepared. You're going to see offensive things; you just don't look at it. You have to look at somebody's face,' she says.

Potential volunteers need to be prayed for and prepared. 'You have to ask people, "Is this going to stir something up for you, some issue that doesn't need to be stirred up?"' Ellen says. A friend and her husband were into porn before they became believers. Although this friend would like to join them on outreach in the clubs, she's not ready. 'I've had people say, "I'll never go in there, but I can make cookies and pray for you,"' Ellen says.

'I've never been in a strip-club and I don't have any tatoos, so how could I relate to the women?' I asked Ellen, 'Would the right outfit help?'

'If God wants you in there, he's picking you, no matter what,' she told me. Once, a grandmother accompanied her team into the clubs, which the women there loved. 'I think a lot of girls like me because I'm the mom who goes in and talks to them when their own mom doesn't,' Ellen said. All of the women she's talked to have suffered from absentee mothers.

Many women confess to being very promiscuous to Ellen, but 'they always add, "I just want to be held, I'm just so lonely." They are in such need of an authentic relationship with our King, as we are.'[14]

Although the ministry is often slow, in three recent months, Ellen witnessed four women stop working in the clubs. Her friends and church have prayed for them by name. 'Prayers are pushing back the gates of hell and making a difference!' she writes. 'Pray that God will do for them what He did for me, what He did for YOU, what He wants to do for all of them – pluck them out of the trash and redeem them for HIS glory.'[15]

ONE STEP FURTHER

Read: Matthew 21:28–33, the parable of the two sons.

Reflect: Jesus says those who enter the kingdom of God accept his invitation by their words and actions. The prostituted man or woman or their abusers may be more ready to follow God than the person who has grown up going to church every Sunday. What would you have done in Tanya's shoes when Harmony confessed she was a stripper?

Pray: Do you pass any strip clubs or lap-dancing clubs regularly? Whisper a prayer for the men and women inside, that God sends someone to incarnate Christ's love to them.

CHAPTER 11

Prodigal Sons: Men in Prostitution

I first heard about John Green's ministry to men in prostitution at a conference in Wisconsin. Compelled by his words, one autumn day I visited him at Emmaus Ministries in downtown Chicago to learn how his team welcomes men from the streets into a loving community.[1]

'When I first saw men in prostitution, I thought, "Dude, why don't you get a job?"' John Green admits. He grew up in a wealthy suburb of Akron, Ohio, on a 100-acre private lake and served as an altar boy in a large Roman Catholic parish. When John was 16, his parents gave him a 16-foot sailboat as a Confirmation gift. 'I thought every kid my age had a sailboat,' he says.

Later, two years spent with a homeless youth ministry in New York City revealed the cruelty of street life to John. He began asking how to live justly, show mercy and walk humbly with God (Micah 6:8). These questions led him back to Wheaton College and Graduate School, while he began reaching out to the most ostracized among Chicago's homeless people – prostituting men.

In 1990, John launched Emmaus Ministries, an evangelical Catholic–Protestant outreach that incarnates Christ's love to prostituted men. Andy (see Chapter 4) and about forty other men each month enjoy reprieve from the streets' lies in the basement drop-in center. There Andy finds hot showers, laundry facilities, home-cooked meals, Bible studies, and people like the founder John Green, who care whether he lives or dies.

Today, John, 43, directs the ministry in a three-story former crack-house in Chicago's Uptown neighborhood. Behind the aging brick building, John and his wife Carolyn live in a condo with their three boys (ages 1, 3 and 5). Where drugs once fed empty lives, the Emmaus team shows God's love to the city's forgotten people.

Five nights a week, teams from Emmaus scour gritty urban streets. Pairs of men and women offer men hot coffee, cookies and an invitation to the Emmaus drop-in center.

Lindsay Myers loiters in 'Boys' Town' on most nights until 3 a.m., hoping to develop friendships with hustlers, who are predominantly African-American in Chicago. She and three other recent college graduates are volunteering at Emmaus full-time for one year in exchange for room, board and $20 a week.

'I love this work because I feel like this is where Jesus would be,' the 23-year-old Florida native tells me. 'There's nothing we can do that's ever gonna change these guys. It's God's work.'

Uniting the Body

Both volunteers and staff appreciate how the ministry's joint Protestant and Catholic outreach unites them. 'Emmaus is a great chance for humility,' says Ronnie LaGrow, who graduated from a private Catholic college. 'Your eyes are opened to all these Christians serving. There's such friendship and an underlying joy we share.'

John Green's desire to heal divisions in the church developed from defending his faith as a minority Catholic among Wheaton College's Protestant student population. He discovered that misconceptions abounded among both Catholics and Protestants.

When John married Carolyn, the daughter of an American Baptist pastor, the couple committed to building unity in the Body of Christ by serving the poor. An ordained Catholic deacon, John believes that 'If we work together with integrity and we do it well, there's some real healing in the Body.'

The power of presence

Once a month on Saturday afternoons, Paul Horcher, 46, leaves his wife and six children to battle the traffic into Chicago. At Emmaus, Paul and other volunteers join the men who drop by for a family-style meal and maybe watch a movie. 'It took me a long time to realize that hanging out is very important,' Paul says. 'I think the guys realize that volunteers like me don't have to be there, and that's telling them, "You know, I must be worth something for him to show up."'

A former dairy farmer and the owner of a suburban construction company, Paul finds city life foreign. But three years ago the Archdiocese of Chicago challenged him to stretch his faith through a service project. He chose Emmaus.

Now Paul looks forward to these Saturdays. 'We meet Christ when we engage the broken,' he says. 'These men tend to be very gentle people and their opportunities have been limited to none. At Emmaus they can let down their street mask, they're safe and nobody is judging them.'

The hospitality, consistent friendship, prayer and discipleship at Emmaus embody Christ's unconditional love. 'One of our guys recently told me, "Emmaus was for me what the telephone booth was to Superman – a place to change,"' John says.

God's instrument

Jim found the boost he needed to overcome his addictions and stop prostituting in 1999, thanks to Emmaus. Now on Wednesday mornings in the softly-lit chapel room, he leads a popular men's Bible study. A large framed print of Rembrandt's *The Return of the Prodigal Son* hangs prominently, a reminder of God's mercy.

Jim empathizes with Andy and seven other men present. 'I don't want anyone to think I'm better than you. I'm just a little better than I used to be,' he tells them. 'Temptation is consistently bombarding me.'

His hair is flecked with gray, and at 55, Jim may be the oldest man there. Both his testimony and age command respect.

Later Jim pulls a wad of folded bills from his jeans to show me. 'I have money in my pocket and no desire for drugs. I feel good when I wake up in the morning. I ask God, "Make me an instrument to do your will."'

Most volunteers can't identify so well with the men's brokenness, including Lindsay. 'I see our guys as so different from me, but I want to see how we're equal before God,' she says. 'In the Book of Hosea we're all harlots before God – we sell ourselves to other things.'

Walking together

Emmaus Ministries hasn't given up on Andy, but he's still chained to his addictions. Today Andy is paying a high price with AIDS. His body is falling apart – he can barely walk two blocks without sitting down.

John and his team are waiting patiently for a breakthrough. 'We are a place of faith where Andy can be honest with his struggles. I'm willing to journey with him,' John says. 'God incarnated himself into our world in the midst of all our humanness and crud. He came, was present and he walked with us.'

Andy's longing for peace may foreshadow the transformation that John's team has prayed for. 'I'm really tired of the whole thing,' he told me recently over the phone. 'I just want some peace – inner peace, outer peace, physical peace.'

ONE STEP FURTHER

Read: Mark 1:40–45: Jesus heals the man with leprosy.

Reflect: Jesus offered the leper a great example of the 'three Ts' of ministry: time, touch and talk. These three basic elements enable all of us to socialize well and be comfortable with who and what we are. It can be overwhelming to help society's outcasts figure out who and what they are, and their place in the world. We in the church need to keep it simple: give them what Jesus gave the leper – time, touch and talk – and allow the Holy Spirit room to work.[2]

Pray: That God would help you overcome any prejudices or fears you may have toward men in prostitution. Pray that God would reveal to you any doubts or disdain about ministering with others in Christ's Body who are different from yourself.

'The Streets I Feared to See'

I said: 'Let me walk in the field.' God said: 'Nay, walk
in the town.'
I said: 'There are no flowers there.' He said: 'No
flowers but a crown.'
I said: 'But the sky is black and there is nothing but
noise and din.'
But He wept as He sent me back, 'There is more,' He
said, 'there is sin.'
I said: 'But the air is thick and fogs are veiling the sun.'
He answered: 'Yet souls are sick, and souls in the dark
undone.'
I said: 'I shall miss the light, and friends will miss me,
they say.'
He answered me: 'Choose tonight, if I am to miss you,
or they.'
I pleaded for time to be given; He said: 'Is it hard to
decide?
It will not seem hard in Heaven, to have followed the
steps of your guide.'
I cast one look at the fields, then set my face to the
town.
He said: 'My child, do you yield? Will you leave the
flowers for the crown?'
Then into His hand went mine, and into my heart came
He;
And I walk in a light Divine, the streets I had feared to
see.

George McDonald (1824–1905)

CHAPTER 12

Loving the Least of These: Transgendered People

I met Roberto in São Paulo, Brazil, last November in a group home run by CENA (Comunidade Evangélica Nova Aurora).[1] After we breakfasted, the house supervisor, Paulo, asked if anyone wanted to share their testimony with me. That afternoon in the quiet living-room, Roberto eagerly told me his story of redemption, as Paulo translated.

Roberto was prostituting himself as a transvestite in São Paolo's infamous Luz neighborhood to earn cash for his next crack smoke (see Chapter 4). One day he was eating lunch with other transvestites when they spoke highly of a staff worker from CENA, a ministry to homeless people and prostituting men and women in São Paulo. Curious, Roberto soon had a chance to meet the pastor. He accepted an invitation to go camping with the ministry. For two days, Roberto and other transvestites enjoyed the green countryside, heard about Jesus' unconditional love and forgiveness, and got to know the CENA staff.

When they returned to the city, Roberto had lost his homosexual feelings. 'I didn't want to have sex any more or to live with other transvestites,' he says. 'We used drugs, but inside I had changed. My wish was to live with God's people.'

At 2 a.m. in the morning, he called Paolo Cappelletti, then director of CENA, for help. Paolo told Roberto to come to the ministry office. There Roberto met Paolo and several other staff, and repeated his wishes for a changed life.

The next day Roberto boarded a bus and headed to the ministry's farm in Juquitiba, several hours from São Paolo. On the farm's 20 hectares (50 acres), about 60 men, women and children were learning to live in Christian community. The adults farmed the land, caring for the vegetable garden and the banana plantation, practiced carpentry and learned new vocational skills. But within a few days, Roberto's dreams for a sex change returned to haunt him. After only twelve days, he decided to return to the city, although he promised himself that he would return to the farm someday.

Four years passed before Roberto returned. During that time, he sank into deeper darkness, dealing and using drugs, and doing more prostitution. 'But I didn't get anywhere,' he says. Still, he knew someday he would return to the farm.

A four-month stint in the squalor of a São Paulo jail pushed Roberto to choose between heaven and hell. 'I saw hell in prison – fighting, drugs and prostitution,' he says. Desperate, one day he cried out to God, 'What do you want me to do?'

He heard the Lord reply, 'When you leave here, go back to the farm.'

Roberto promised, 'If you set me free, I will go to the farm.' Reassured by God's answer, he prayed each day in his cell and clung to hope in Jesus.

But when he was released on probation, Roberto immediately returned to his old friends in the Luz neighborhood, also known as 'Crackland'. He spent the next eight days getting high with street addicts. But each day he also heard God whisper, 'I freed you, but you aren't keeping your promise.'

Satan also had a grip on Roberto. 'I saw the devil walking around me, although he didn't touch me,' he says.

On the eighth day out of prison, 'I raised my hands and prayed, "Help me, Father. Forget my sins, and help me."' When his addict friends heard Roberto cry, 'Help me' aloud, they offered him more drugs. He refused. Instead, he prayed, 'Help me. I never want to use drugs again or be a homosexual.'

Roberto removed his wig and his dress, and then stopped smoking crack with the help of a CENA staff member. The following week he returned to the farm.

Over the next year, Roberto battled with his old desires for drugs and prostitution, but he was also drawn to the Christian community and serving God. He dreaded returning to the city and the temptations he'd encounter there. Worries about being stigmatized by his old transvestite friends plagued him.

One day in chapel service, Roberto heard a Bible message about how God had promised Hannah, Samuel's mother, a son. He was reminded of God's faithfulness to keep his promises and felt peace about his own uncertain future.

After a year and four months, Roberto moved back to São Paolo and into a group home, supervised by Paolo and his family. 'Instead of transvestites and drug dealers, God prepared a new place for me,' he says.

Roberto committed to his new life when he agreed to plastic surgery to remove the silicon on his breasts and buttocks. He still enjoyed feeling like a woman, but God told him, 'I have a test for you. Remove the silicon and I'll provide something else for you.' Suddenly Roberto grasped the meaning of leaving the old behind and becoming a new creation in Christ (2 Corinthians 5:17).

One year later, Roberto still lives in Paolo's group home with eighteen other men and women. 'I thank God because I have a family now – this house,' says Roberto. He is taking classes toward a high school diploma and plans to enroll in college classes someday.

Roberto and another former transvestite regularly visit and share the gospel with a group of transvestites who live and prostitute nearby. 'I'm sad because they don't see Jesus,' he says. 'I pray that the other transvestites look at me and see that God can change them. They think it's impossible, but I know they have a chance and can change.'

In the sprawling cities of São Paulo, Athens, Chicago and beyond, God's people are defying centuries-old stigmas and offering Christ's love to transgendered people and prostituted men, often society's most forgotten people.

'If we see a guy on the street, and he's filthy or he smells bad, and he comes up and wants a hug, I'm gonna hug him,' says Sil Davis of Emmaus Ministries in Chicago.[2] Sil's best intentions were challenged one night by a transvestite whose hormone use went awry. Sil exited the 'L' (Chicago's raised subway) at 95th Street, and a familiar voice greeted him. 'He wanted a hug. I had a choice: either I stop five minutes, and that will show him more than one hour of counseling that I love him because I'm not ashamed of him, or... That's the kind of love we want to show.'

Outreach to transvestites has become more difficult over the years as societies have become more tolerant of homosexuals. 'They used to wear wigs and Lee press-on nails. Now some take hormones and their breasts are their own. They get nails cemented on,' Sil says.

'They see themselves as being born women, just trapped in a man's body. It's hard for us because the recovery community supports that.' In Chicago, transsexuals can attend transgender

AA meetings or get free hormones from another non-profit organization.

'Sissy talk' and dressing in drag is not allowed inside the Emmaus building. 'They take on personas to survive,' Sil says, but he sees their behaviors change at Emmaus. 'Some guys have been molested as children. They learned that being a man wasn't safe.' So the ministry offers a safe place where the men are free to become more masculine, unlike the world outside where they worry about how they are perceived – even how they sit or cross their legs.

Although Roberto embraced his masculinity while surrounded by supportive Christians, it's normal for other redeemed men to struggle for years with homosexual feelings. A caring community and accountability are critical to helping them live as men in their true identity.

Emmaus and other ministries aim to offer holistic care for men and women in prostitution. Besides a spiritual solution to problems, they also need caring friendships, just laws, housing, adequate medical care, access to drug rehab programs, vocational training, new jobs and more.

Nea Zoi's volunteer manual states: 'We are committed to providing holistic care, motivated by the full meaning of salvation, which includes physical, emotional, relational and spiritual well being. We recognize that as we love the women and men we meet in practical ways, we are preparing the way for restoration to relationship with a loving heavenly Father.'[3]

Volunteers at Nea Zoi met Manuel, 43, as he was working the streets as a transvestite. 'We talked with him for over a year about his addictions, his spiritual needs, and his health needs. At one point, we realized that he had very severe myopia and had lost his glasses. We were able to arrange an eye exam and secure new glasses for him. This seemed to be a key for him, and within a month, he made a decision to enter a drug rehabilitation program.'[4]

That first encounter

Every Thursday night in Athens, teams of volunteers with Nea Zoi go out in pairs to Syngrou Street, where they approach prostituted women and transvestites. Myrto Theocharous, a volunteer from Cyprus (see Chapter 8), told me about her first encounter with a transvestite:[5]

'We were standing on the sidewalk. I saw a very tall person with long boots and big blonde hair, smoking and walking up and down. I was terrified. "Oh, my God. What are we gonna do, what are we gonna say?" I thought.

'Emma [Nea Zoi's director] grabbed me. We crossed to the woman's side of the road. Emma said, "Hi, this is my friend, Myrto." The woman said, "Hi, where are you from?" and asked me about Cyprus.

'I noticed she was trying to make me comfortable. I thought, "This isn't that bad. She's not a monster, she's a person." Then I noticed this person wasn't a woman but a man – there was a roughness in the voice and facial features. Emma had told me earlier that they might be a transvestite. Why was I so afraid of this person?

'I realized I feared myself more than her. I feared my reaction – that I wouldn't have God's mercy in my heart and wouldn't approach this person as they deserved. I realized the problem wasn't the person, but it was me. I thought I'd fall short of God's expectations. God's mercy and heart for these people is so big… God doesn't look at the outer person. I knew I was so limited, I would look at the outside.

'That first encounter broke the ice for me. After that I felt more free to approach them. People don't look down on me and say, "What do you want?" They're not aggressive. My image of prostituting women and transvestites was shattered. I saw they were very friendly, they want to meet people too, and they care.'

ONE STEP FURTHER

Read: Isaiah 54:4: 'Do not be afraid; you will not suffer shame. Do not fear disgrace; you will not be humiliated.'

Reflect: God's redemptive love is free of condemnation. He does not require that we change our behavior before coming to him. The Holy Spirit prompts us to conform to God's ways only after we are in relationship with God.

Roberto was rejected by his own family and yearned for the kind of love that God's family offered. Is your church community a place where people like Roberto would be received with love? Or would society's stigmas prevail there? Would you welcome him before he had the silicon removed from his body?

Pray: For God to create in your heart and your community the love and acceptance God desires to show to broken men and women.

CHAPTER 13

Healing Solutions

'Forgiveness'

Can forgiveness be good or bad?
Can it make us happy or just really sad?
I don't know, I've not learnt the art,
Of forgiving people that have ripped me apart.
I've never been good at letting things go,
When others just seem to go with the flow,
I hold things right down deep inside,
And walk about pretending to be full of pride.
But I have no pride and no forgiveness,
I've never been treated like some little princess,
No one has ever put my life at ease,
So why the f— should I live to please?
So forgiveness what is it? How does it work?
When all my life has been full of hurt,
But I'm still here to live another day,
And hope the art of forgiveness comes my way.

Cara, April 2007[1]

Trauma counseling for recent trafficking victims is still a great need around the world, says Kathy Stout-LaBauve, LCSW, trafficking aftercare specialist for International Justice Mission

(IJM). Kathy visited seventeen aftercare homes in four countries, where none of the girls she spoke with appeared to understand the dynamics of trafficking, nor was trafficking addressed in any of the daily schedules, activities or groups she observed.[2]

Kathy talked about the emotional and physical obstacles victims face in the early stages of their rehabilitation. 'There's more shame attached to sexual trauma in the developing world,' Kathy says. 'There is still very much a "blame the victim" mentality and a contributing factor to this is the Buddhist and Hindu belief in karma: "That's just what I was born into and what I deserve, so what's the point of talking about it, because that's just my life."'

A veteran therapist for victims of sexual trauma, Kathy is developing a framework for model care that IJM's thirty-plus partnering aftercare homes can modify and implement. Understanding trauma and facilitating recovery is a key component. She hopes that all programs will include trauma recovery counseling.

Initially, when trafficking survivors are rescued, they are frightened. But once they reach a safe aftercare home, they can move out of survival mode. Kathy describes the classic signs of trauma that appear initially: 'Nightmares and flashbacks, which are like watching a movie in your head – with the adrenaline rushes and rapid heartbeat that accompanied the actual experience. The survivor's body is in a startled reaction all the time. She goes from that to a numbing response, as if she is walking around in a dazed state.' Some survivors have amnesia for the experiences they suffered, because what happened was just too overwhelming. Memory may return slowly.

Initial counseling entails developing rapport and a safe relationship, then teaching skills for managing painful feelings, rather than starting to unravel details of the trauma too soon. 'You may show them how to feel something that's uncomfortable, then teach them how to get out of it. You're giving them a dimmer switch... they can turn the light up or down,' Kathy says. With these skills, trauma survivors can talk about a painful event, and then move out of it rather than acting out in self-destructive behavior such as cutting themselves.

The next phase is trauma resolution, where a survivor explores the trauma and, over time, integrates it into her life rather than keeping it separate from the rest of her life experience. This stage requires pacing, much care and a professional counselor, Kathy says. Therapeutic techniques include writing letters to perpetrators or parents (if they were involved), using acting to express feelings, and cognitive-behavioral processing. Artwork can also be a tool for expressing feelings that are difficult to express in words.

As the dynamics of the trafficking situation are talked about, the person will grasp more deeply how it affected her. 'Hopefully she'll develop empathy for herself as a trafficking survivor and begin to see herself not as damaged goods but as a precious child of God. That will replace the shame,' Kathy says.

She describes the last phase of trauma work as examining and making positive choices in all the areas of life that were affected – spirituality, femininity, relationships, sexuality. 'You begin to make different choices, feel better about yourself and no longer feel ashamed. You make better decisions about relationships with people who respect you and treat you well because you understand you're worthy of respect.'

The time-frame for healing varies greatly with each person, but trauma therapy should be strategic and focused. 'These girls have been treated so thoughtlessly, we need to put all our energy into treating them thoughtfully with recovery as our goal,' Kathy says.

Although some cultures in Asia do not encourage the sharing of feelings and thoughts with others, Kathy has repeatedly observed that girls 'were almost bursting to tell their stories to counselors they trusted.'

'People want to share their trauma and get help working through it, no matter what part of the world they live in,' Kathy says. 'I think we are created to seek healing solutions, no matter what culture we live in.'

Diving for the deepest pearl

Many counseling programs in the Philippines lean toward a Western approach – in a clinic or a private room. But often effective counseling can be informal, Thelma says. The founder of Samaritana, a ministry to prostituted women in the Philippines, she has a Masters in Counseling and uses both approaches.[3]

Volunteers at Samaritana learn that the ministry's top principle is listening and having a learner's attitude, starting where the women are. Also key is understanding how 'God views people, what dignity entails, and what it means for these women to be born with potential,' says Thelma. A good listener can help a woman get in touch with her God-given potential and give her hope.

Thelma helps women discover they are created in the image of God by respecting them, affirming their sadness, and 'diving for the deepest pearl in their lives' – signs of a person's true identity. The pearls surface as she listens. One woman who struggled to feed herself and her baby gave her last cup of rice to another woman with two children. She told Thelma, 'I drank water, ate three crackers, and I had a little milk for my baby. I'm still alive.'

Thelma connected this woman's experience to the biblical example of the widow who gave her last coin at the temple. She makes it a practice to connect their stories to Scripture by asking, 'Did you know there's a story in the Bible of someone who did something similar?'

The women's stories of endurance through suffering are opportunities to affirm them. 'These girls say profound things to me. The Bible says, "from the mouths of babes come deepest praises."'[4] She tells them, 'You're a very courageous person for being able to stand that trial' or 'I learned from you how to trust God for my needs.'

Developing self-worth

Pierre Tami, president of Hagar International, says developing women's self-esteem is key to their recovery from fear. Professional counseling and therapy at Hagar Cambodia help traumatized women identify their coping mechanisms – how they've survived great suffering.[5]

Discovering this ability to cope is integral to developing self-worth. 'If a woman has been gang-raped or forced to sleep in a brothel, she won't just trust anyone. This fear must be removed, but you can't say, "Don't worry, honey, don't be afraid." This has to be replaced with something – the ability to cope and have self-worth. Otherwise she won't be able to do any job – sew, cook, or whatever.'

Christian values play an integral role in developing a woman's self-identity, Pierre believes. In Cambodia's Buddhist context, karma dictates life's circumstances and fails to offer hope to suffering women. Christians make a huge difference, because 'We believe we are created in the image and likeness of God, and life has sanctity and worth,' Pierre says.

ONE STEP FURTHER

Read: Isaiah 49:13–15:

Shout for joy, O heavens; rejoice, O earth; burst into
  song, O mountains!
For the LORD comforts his people and will have compassion on his afflicted ones.
But Zion said, 'The LORD has forsaken me, the LORD
  has forgotten me.'
'Can a mother forget the baby at her breast and have
  no compassion on the child she has borne?
Though she may forget, I will not forget you!'

Reflect: Accepting comfort and love can be hard for those
who have been betrayed and wounded. Have you ever had
difficulty trusting God or others after being hurt? Have you
had any opportunities to comfort others because you've
experienced similar pain?

Pray: That God provides more skilled counselors and people who can help bring healing into the lives of men and
women whose identities and lives have been twisted by
sexual exploitation.

CHAPTER 14

Celebrating the Little Things:
Discipleship

Estelle Blake is passionate about bringing people closer to Jesus one by one through Faith House, the Salvation Army's small outreach center for prostituted women and men in London's King Cross area. Faith House is several doorsteps from a bustling Burger King near the tube stop. I almost overlooked the small white sign hanging over the doorway, crowded among many offices lining the side street.[1]

Mary was still prostituting herself as she served time in London's Holloway prison for women. She sold her body for drugs and food to other female prisoners. Estelle Blake, manager of Faith House, met Mary on a chaplaincy visit to the prison. She relayed their conversation to me:

Mary: 'Estelle, I really want to choose Jesus, but do you think he'll help me face the shit and the crap in my life? 'Cause I chose Buddha, and Buddha says it's my fault.

'And I tried out not believing in God, but I kept asking God where he was and telling him I didn't believe in him anymore. But there's no point in my being an atheist if I keep telling him he doesn't exist, because then I believe he exists. And I tried all these other different faiths.'

Estelle: 'Why do you want to choose Jesus?'

Mary: 'Because I think he might be the one who'll help me. But will he take all the shit away?'

Estelle: 'No, he can't take it away.'

Mary: 'Oh, well, that's a waste of time, isn't it?'

Estelle: 'No. The difference is that Jesus will walk with you into the shit. And if you walk into it and you're trying to sort it out, you won't be on your own sorting it out. You'll have another friend, another person to help you through it.'

Mary: 'Miss, that's what I've been looking for. That's what I've wanted. What do I do to ask Jesus to walk with me into the shit and the crap? Can you tell me what to say?'

Estelle: 'Yes. [She leads Mary in a prayer of repentance and ends it with:] Dear Jesus, help my friend as she walks into the shit and the crap with you walking beside her. Amen.'

Mary: 'Miss, that was the best f—ing prayer anyone's ever f—ing said to me!'

Estelle never saw Mary again, but she continues to pray for her and hopes she's not dead. 'Those are the little things we celebrate and get excited about,' she tells me. 'For Mary, for the first time in her life, somebody had been honest with her.'

King's Cross is London's cheapest neighborhood for purchasing commercial sex. Homelessness, drug and alcohol addictions, and violence are not uncommon. One woman told Estelle, 'There are only three ways to get out of King's Cross: you go to prison, you go to rehab, or you go out in a coffin.'

When Estelle surveyed prostituting women in King's Cross about their greatest needs, she heard the same feedback again and again: 'You can get food, you can get clothing, you can get money if you need it, you can get somewhere to stay. The one thing you can't get is someone to sit and talk with you about Jesus and pray with you.' Many women Estelle meets on her street walks come from church backgrounds and want to pray and talk. The center offers drop-in times for meals, snacks, discussion and prayer integrated through it all. Currently, a weekly group studies the Ten Commandments.

Many women are slow to trust Jesus. 'A lot of women have issues with Christianity because their abuse came in the name of God,' Estelle says. One woman she knows was abused by a priest, 'because she was a naughty girl.' Another woman's punishment as a girl was being forced to read the Bible.

At least 95 per cent of the women Estelle knows in King's Cross have been sexually abused, she says. Helping them understand that it's okay to be angry with God is critical to their discipleship. Ultimately, she aims to prove that 'Christianity is about everyday reality,' walking with God through life's ups and downs, and is not limited to inside church walls.

'We praise God for the little things that happen,' Estelle says. 'If a woman comes back to Faith House a second time, it means the first time we made her feel important enough to want to come back. It means she trusted us enough to come back a second time.'

Estelle also celebrates the big things – when God heals, and the women see that God both hears and answers their prayers:

'My boss was here one day for our discussion and prayer group,' says Estelle. 'We'd just had our thought and our discussion. And then I said, "Does anybody want to pray?" Helen sat in the corner. She had an abscess in her tooth that was so huge, her whole face was swollen. Her boyfriend had cleaned an abscess out in her head with his own fingers – the scar and the scab and the muck...

'One woman in our group who was illiterate said, "I think we should pray for Helen." So, I said, "Okay, then what shall we do?" She put her hand on Helen and said, "Well, I put my hand on her, don't I, because that reminds me who I'm praying for and it reminds God who I'm praying for." I'm thinking, "Well, she's kind of got it, but not quite, but that's okay." So I said, "Well, we have a philosophy that if you say it, you pray it." 'Cause we want to teach the women it's not about flowery language and the person being a minister, it's about you expressing yourself and who you are and what you are to God.

'She puts her hands on Helen and says, "Dear Jesus, I want you to bless Helen, because she's got a bugger of a toothache and it's giving her bleeding gyp. And we'd be most bloody grateful if you could heal her, in your bleeding name. Amen."

'The next day Helen went to the doctor, and he said, "Your head is a clean scalp, there are no signs of wounds, scabs, ulcers or anything on your head." Then she went to the dentist for her toothache, and he said she had the best set of teeth he'd ever seen – no signs of abscess, weakness or anything. He said, "You're wasting my time coming here." Helen came back and told us, so we had a party.

'We celebrate the small things. That proved it's not the language we use, it's as much about coming to God as we are.'

God's active pursuit

Thelma Nambu's counseling insights and contemplative spirituality have helped many women draw closer to God at Samaritana, a ministry to prostituted women in the Philippines. Emotional healing and spiritual growth are not isolated to participation in Bible study or counseling, but integrated in daily life as women read Scripture together, pray, sing, cook, clean, learn handicrafts, and talk in group and one-on-one counseling sessions.[2]

Since the Philippines is a predominantly Catholic country, many women considered themselves Christians already, although they may lack a conscious or animated personal relationship with Christ. On Friday mornings, the women gather for an extended time of Bible study, discussion and reflection on Scripture. They follow the Catholic Bible reading schedule, taking turns to read Scripture aloud. Thelma believes that the Word and choruses they read and sing become God's redeeming tools in their hearts.

Silence also plays a big role in devotions at Samaritana. Thelma invites the women to 'come into the silence where Jesus is waiting, and experience his love in their hearts.' At prayer time, she asks women how they prefer to pray – in silence or aloud.

Listening is core to the women discovering God's presence in their lives. Thelma defines the discipleship process as 'helping people become aware that God is actively pursuing us, and is in community with us. It's helping the person identify, appreciate, and respond to the reality that God is actually doing something in us. They discover this as they learn to listen.'

Recognizing each woman's dignity, potential and gifting is key to offering her hope and glimpses of our Creator, Thelma affirms. 'Evangelicals emphasize being born sinful,' she says, but in spite of human depravity, there is God's abiding presence. The women who come to Samaritana already bear heavy burdens of shame and sin for their involvement in commercial sexual exploitation.

'I believe the thing is to live as a Christian, speaking the words of Jesus in ways they can understand in their struggles,' Thelma says.

Evangelicals tend to be impatient sometimes, she says. 'They put God in a box. If you go to church, tithe, and so on, you're a Christian. But that's not growth.

'Some evangelicals ask me, "Are the women converted? Did they receive Jesus? Have you heard them say the sinner's prayer?" They're so preoccupied with that. I'm not de-emphasizing our depraved nature, but in spite of it, there is the potential and gifting God has given us.' Thelma measures the women's spiritual growth as she sees them learning to trust God in daily life.

Lorie used to be quiet and afraid to share about her life, for fear of what others might think. One Sunday, she was helping to sell Samaritana's handicrafts at a local church after a worship service. People asked her what Samaritana does and how she became part of it. One woman who listened to Lorie was encouraged because she had a similar past. 'I realize how God is using my story to connect with others, and this has encouraged me to tell my story as the situation calls for it,' Lorie said.[3]

Lorie, who is skilled in handicrafts, now helps teach crafts to new women trainees at Samaritana's center. She also talks with women working in bars during night outreaches.

Resurrecting dreams

Edna Vallenilla has been visiting prostituting women in Amsterdam's central red-light district since 2003 with The Cleft, a YWAM ministry. Twice a week she and a small team serve coffee, tea and cookies to the women standing behind brothel windows for long eight-hour shifts.[4]

A missionary from Venezuela, Edna and her Mexican colleague reach out to Spanish-speaking women, mostly from the Dominican Republic, Ecuador and Colombia. Most Latino women they meet come to Amsterdam out of economic desperation. Their families back home become their 'pimps'. 'Their dreams are broken – to have families, a profession. Something happened in their family – their father left, they're the sole support for their brothers and sisters, and so on,' she says. 'If they found another way to support their families with dignity, they'd prefer it.' Most of the women keep prostitution a secret from family back home.

Edna invites many women to Bible studies, but few come. Many say, 'When I'm clean and not doing this work, I'll come.' She urges them to come now. 'The women don't feel worthy in front of God. They feel like hypocrites,' she says. 'This is a lie from the enemy because the only one who can make us clean is the Lord.'

Building trust with the women takes time and the Spirit's guidance. 'If you push their boundaries, they feel abused,' Edna says. One woman told her, 'You know, I like it when you come because you're the only person who comes to give, not to get.'

Edna gets frustrated with the slow results. 'But the Lord tells me, "I send you to show my love and not to do anything else. Know them as a person, hear their private pain, pray for them."'

Sometimes the women she knows beckon her to their windows and ask her to pray. Some have prayed to receive Christ with Edna, but then they disappear and she never sees them again.

After four years of consistent outreach, Edna has begun to see significant change among six women. Four have left prostitution after meeting the Lord. For the last six months, two women have been coming to Edna's weekly bilingual Bible study and prayer time. One of the women recently told Edna she heard the Lord speaking to her. 'I'm so in love with him. I really want to know him more,' she said.

God is working in their hearts, Edna says. 'The Lord is the only one who can resurrect their dreams and restore them… I cannot force them [to leave prostitution]. They have families to support and they need to trust the Lord for that,' she says. 'I have no money to give them if they stop.'

Edna has developed close friendships with some of the women. 'For me, they're persons and we start to become friends. We share our burdens and dreams.' They meet for coffee, go shopping, watch movies and go to the beach together.

'I'm no martyr,' Edna says. 'I enjoy what the Lord asks me to do. God is really good.'

She also invites women to accompany her to 'The Healing Room', a non-denominational prayer ministry that meets on Mondays in the red-light district and is open to anyone who wants prayer for healing in their life. Some women have started to go for prayer on their own and bring their friends. 'Every time we pray, we worship, it's like a little step toward the Lord,' Edna says.

ONE STEP FURTHER

Read: Luke 24:13–32, the Road to Emmaus.

Reflect: Jesus walks with two unsuspecting believers who discuss their disappointment after the Messiah's death. Instead of revealing his identity immediately, Jesus takes the time to explain the Scriptures, walk and dine with them.

Women and men who've been sexually exploited face immense obstacles in trusting others and believing in God's goodness. They require people with Christ-like patience to walk with them through their hardships and reveal Jesus' love in both word and deed.

Pray: Ask God to give you a heart of patience for those whom God calls you to disciple. Pray for the staff and volunteers at Faith House, the Cleft and Samaritana to be effective witnesses of God's love.

CHAPTER 15

Change Takes Time

I met Julia* in São Paolo, Brazil. A Brazilian of Japanese descent, she looked like one of my aunts with her black bob and petite frame. I tried out my Japanese on her and managed to win an ounce of trust, in part through our shared heritage.[1]

Julia was 15 when she was raped by a group of boys at her high school. They shoved her in a car and bruised her neck while forcing themselves on her. 'I was very afraid for a long time,' she recalls. Julia visited a hospital because of the excruciating pain and inflammation in her vagina, but she never told her mother what had happened. The two didn't get along, and her mother beat Julia to discipline her even as a teen.

At 20, Julia left home and found herself in a neighborhood in São Paolo known for drugs and prostitution. The old plaza called Republic Square is surrounded by porn theaters featuring X-rated flicks, 'cafes' that open for business at 10 p.m., seedy bars where customers and prostituting women discuss price, and the hotels where they may go next.[2] In Brazil, prostitution is not illegal, but pimping is, so fronts for commercial sex are ample.

The entrance of the 'American Bar' is decorated with red, blue and white balloons. The customer climbs eighteen steps,

143

and through a glass door sees images of couples engaged in all kinds of sex flickering across a big screen.[3]

Not far from here is the Luz area, where Julia found herself. Invited into an apartment building, she met many women. At first she didn't realize it was a brothel, and that a woman in the building was pimping all the other women living there. 'I didn't know then that the world can devour people,' she told me.

Julia learned the 'trade' quickly. 'I was new, pretty, and I made a lot of money although I was infected,' she told me. The other women encouraged her to spend her money with them at bars, drinking and dancing. 'I thought everything was okay. I had money and I enjoyed myself,' she says.

Fifteen years passed in the brothel before Julia was thrown out onto the streets, and began prostituting in cheap hotels. On the street, she met Paolo Cappelletti, then director of CENA, a ministry devoted to reaching homosexuals, transvestites and prostituted women and men. For eight years, Paolo shared the gospel with Julia. And for eight years, Julia ignored him. 'I thought it was nonsense. He talked about Jesus, but every time I had another reason why I didn't want to seek Jesus. I was drinking and smoking cigarettes. I was depressed, I was empty inside.'

But after twenty-three years of selling her body, Julia was tired of suffering. 'I was tired of being a slave of Satan,' she said.

Julia met with social workers at CENA and agreed to spend at least six months at the ministry's farm in the hills of Juquitiba, several hours from São Paulo. There about 60 men, women and children live in Christian community on the farm's 20 hectares (50 acres). Mealtimes, devotions, chores, gardening and classes are all scheduled. The farm is a 'school of life' and offers people a chance to restore their dignity as they meet Christ.

Learning the rules and living with others wasn't easy for Julia. When she refused to wash dishes and scour the big pots, she was disciplined. 'It was very different on the street, I didn't have rules or a schedule,' she says. The process of change is hard for many people, and often they choose to return to street life before completing the minimum six months. But Julia's faith deepened during her two and a half years on the farm as she learned about the gospel and saw it lived out around her.

Today she lives in a group home in São Paulo overseen by Paolo and his family. Six months ago Julia learned she's HIV-positive, which she may have contracted more than six years ago. She knows that she had sex with men infected with AIDS.

Julia has battled depression, but 'Today I'm feeling better, I have more peace,' she tells me. 'Today I have a Father, a good Father and an eternal Father.'

The path of change is not easy. As one Christian publication says: 'It is more difficult for individuals to exit prostitution than to continue.'[4] In Julia's case, the trauma of being gang raped was a significant factor: 'Survivors of sexual abuse will have experienced common factors including traumatic sexualisation, betrayal, powerlessness and stigmatization. Often it is easier to continue in prostitution and mask memories of the past under current behavior, rather than go through the often equally traumatic process of addressing the past and seeking change.'[5]

Other barriers to exiting often include relationships of dependence and intimidation with people involved in pimping and trafficking, and drug addictions.

The change process can be viewed in five stages:[6]

- *Denial to awareness:* Denial serves as a safety mechanism that protects individuals from being overwhelmed by their feelings. They can spend a lot of time in denial, and addictions help them to do that. Progress is moving out of this denial into awareness of the problem.
- *Contemplation:* In this stage, an individual is aware that he/she has a problem and that a change must be made. There will be a willingness to discuss the problem, seeing what needs to change, but no commitment to change.
- *Preparation:* The individual explores ways in which change might occur and chooses the right one.
- *Action:* Here the person makes an attempt for serious change.
- *Maintenance:* In this final stage, there is sustained change over a period of time, which includes change in perspective, attitudes, values and lifestyle, as well as behavior.

Nea Zoi's manual alerts volunteers: 'Relapse occurs frequently at any time, and people can move back and forth between these stages. Our job throughout this process is to accept the individual where they are, and to encourage them, support them and advise them on changes they wish to make. We also want to celebrate any changes they do make! Most often, this process is a matter of years rather than weeks or even months.'[7]

Linda Burkle, who works with the Salvation Army's Wellspring program for women coming out of prostitution in Nebraska, says: 'It's very difficult to leave the lifestyle, because it's a culture. They're not accustomed to keeping appointments, don't have a social security card, any of the things that you need to function in society. They haven't developed a legitimate entrée into regular societal institutions.'[8]

Among the women whom the Wellspring program helps, while incarcerated and after their release, 99 per cent have a substance abuse problem that fuels prostitution. 'Often women get involved in prostitution because of being seduced or enticed into it by a smooth-talking pimp who gets them hooked on drugs. Once they're addicted, they have to keep prostituting to feed the addiction,' Linda says.[9] Crack is their number-one drug of choice.[10]

Once a person is released from the county jail, Wellspring helps provide aftercare, whether temporary housing, treatment for substance abuse and mental health, transportation, counseling, referrals to jobs and vocational training programs.[11]

Sixty to seventy per cent of prostituting people on the street have mental health disorders, says Program Director Mary Raynovich. Many women Wellspring helps have never been diagnosed or prescribed medication to help manage the mental illness, so they self-medicate with drugs and alcohol, Raynovich says. Proper treatment is essential to positive change.[12]

Wellspring serves thirty to forty men and women a month, but there's a chronic cycle from the streets, drugs, prostitution, to jail and back out on the streets. Relapse with drugs or alcohol is common, and occurs even after three to four years. But, 'If it's the tenth time someone has been involved in our program, we never turn anyone away,' Mary says. 'If you're on the street for fifteen years, it doesn't take a year to get off the streets.'[13]

'Normalcy is hard'

The Well is a support house for women exiting the sex industry or at risk of becoming involved. Located on a quiet road in Bristol, England, it provides a rare and much-needed facility. Nearly all the women have had drug or alcohol dependency problems, and some have been incarcerated. At The Well, they feel safe, comfortable and cared about. Leanne writes:

There's nothing like The Well in the town I come from. I'd just come out of prison, after breaching an ASBO (Anti-Social Behavior Order) for prostitution. If I hadn't come here I'd have gone back to a house with other addicts, and straight back on the streets. It's good to be here, but it's a problem to adjust. There's the difficulty of living on far less money than you're used to; my benefit's around £102 for two weeks – I used to earn that in half an hour.

Sometimes I miss life in the fast lane – the night life. I know it sounds stupid but I miss the excitement of meeting punters [men involved in pimping] and not knowing what's going to happen. Getting back to normalcy is hard – doing the same domestic stuff every day, without the excitement.

On the streets I've been robbed, battered, raped – I never knew whether this was the last car I would ever get into, and my parents would get that phone call. Once I had a gun waved in my face. It sounds stupid, but it was exciting. I never thought about the danger at the time, but I did when I was in prison.

So what makes it worthwhile? In the last few months I've been able to have a relationship again with my four children and the rest of my family. I've been going to college, and I've got a boyfriend. The boundaries are there for a reason, and if I've achieved so much in a few months, what can I achieve in two or three years?

It's worth it – that's the message I want to give. It is worth it.[14]

ONE STEP FURTHER

Read: The Book of Hosea.

Reflect: In Hosea, God describes his love in contrast to ours. In Hosea 2:6, God illustrates his deep love for the idolatrous Israelites by trying to prevent Gomer from committing adultery. He blocks her path with thornbushes.

How long was your journey toward God? Were you surprised to read that Julia's journey took eight years to begin?

Despite our wandering ways, God calls us back to himself again and again. Think of two or three ways in which God's love is different to ours?

Pray: That God changes your heart to conform to his.

CHAPTER 16

Working in Freedom

After Moon's rescue from the brothel (see Chapter 1), the Crawfords helped her start a business selling assorted nuts, which didn't pan out. A second effort, selling souvenirs to Thai tourists, proved more profitable. Then, a few months after her rescue, Moon married a Thai man and soon had two babies.[1]

Two years ago, the Crawfords loaned the family $200 for Moon's husband to launch a motorcycle taxi business. The family now earns $5 a day in Myanmar, double the amount they require for food and basic needs.

After years of pouring Jesus' love into the lives of Moon and her young family, the Crawfords' team is witnessing a transformation of her entire family. Moon's husband, who became a Christian four months ago, now reads the Bible to her daily, and local women on the Crawfords' team are teaching Moon to read and write while they disciple her.

Moon, with her knowledge of human trafficking, helps Mark train staff to work with victims of trafficking and exploited street kids. 'I cannot teach reading or writing or help in a lot of ways, but I can use my experience to help other girls like me,' she says. 'I don't want the same thing to happen to them.'

Recently, Moon helped rescue Wan, a 16-year-old girl. Wan was dirty, hungry and wearing a very short skirt while walking the streets near the Thai border. Moon bought her lunch and a soft drink, then heard God telling her to help the girl more.

Wan said her parents had encouraged her to prostitute herself. Minutes before a trafficker arrived to ship Wan to Bangkok, Moon led her to safety at a staff member's house. Moon counseled her during many late nights, and the staff prayed and encouraged Wan until she realized she had other options besides prostitution.

Moon's identity has changed from rescued to rescuer, from victim to counselor, thanks to the Crawfords' ministry and God's redemptive love.

After escaping the devil's bedroom, women and men need help supporting themselves and often their families. 'The story's not over because someone is rescued from a brothel or decides to leave a "bar",' says Christa Crawford. 'It's only beginning.'

Organizations around the world are realizing that vocational training and work opportunities are essential for personal and spiritual restoration. Whether it's through manufacturing handbags in India or producing soya-milk in Cambodia, these organizations help once-broken people discover their full worth in the eyes of Jesus.

The Crawfords realized that few Christian organizations were reaching women who appeared to be 'voluntarily' prostituting in Chiang Mai. So in 2003, the Crawfords decided to pioneer their own outreach, Just Food, Inc., (i.e. 'Justice and Food').

Western-style cafés are popular among locals, the large expatriate and missionary community, and the city's 3 million-plus tourists each year. Christa designed a menu full of the California cuisine she craved, and they opened a modest café housed in a bookstore, featuring items like South-west chicken wraps and tandoori chicken pizza. They trained women – formerly in prostitution and those at risk of entering the trade – to make tor-tillas and gourmet coffee drinks, to serve customers, and to run a kitchen.

Despite the café's enticing menu and décor, some Thai Christians refused to patronize a business tainted by the stigma of prostitution, and many churches have been hesitant to get involved in any way. 'By associating with prostitutes, you're lowering your status,' Mark says. 'It's like working with lepers. Are you going to infect yourself if you're associating with these people?' The Crawfords did help one cutting-edge Thai church to open a day-care facility for children of prostituted women.

In 2004, the Crawfords launched a new venture, a com-bined counseling and vocational training program called Garden of Hope. With Western food still in high demand, Mark and Christa are now raising capital to start a culinary arts academy at their rehabilitation center. The new ministry will reach out to at-risk women, children, and men. In addi-tion to baking and cooking classes, the ministry will offer computer training. The Crawfords anticipate that training for legitimate jobs in restaurants and hotels will fit with the women's gifts. 'These women are [already] in the service industry,' Christa says. 'We need to redeem their skills.'

The Crawfords' views on vocational training were shaped by Mark's years as a training manager for Ritz-Carlton Hotels. 'The emphasis was not correcting people's weaknesses, but playing to their strengths,' he says. With prostitution, 'you're pretending you want to be with someone you don't want to be with. You have to present a false image of yourself,' Mark says. The couple believe that offering multiple training options will help the women and girls discover how God has gifted them and regain a sense of self.

In addition, the women employed at the ministry's garden café will gain customer-service and basic marketing skills. The Crawfords aim to link graduates with jobs and apprenticeships at restaurants and four- or five-star hotels, such as the Four Seasons. Christa hopes to someday supply the four local Starbucks with cinnamon rolls, brownies, and muffins.

The Crawfords also want to turn Just Food, Inc. into a franchise, operating restaurants, bed and breakfasts, and spas where recovering women can gain work skills in supportive environments. This year, they plan to offer loans to thirty women to start micro-enterprise businesses. They're seeking an experienced businessperson to oversee such business development. 'We need most the people who think they are least qualified to be a missionary,' Christa says, 'because often missionaries are the least qualified to start and run successful businesses.'

While their hopes are high, Christa and Mark are not naïve to the challenges of their ministry, especially working with women who often lack formal education and are recovering from sexual exploitation. The miracle, Mark says, occurs when exploited women realize their inherent dignity and need for God. He estimates a transition time of three to five years from life in prostitution to stable work elsewhere, while women grow in Christ and serve in a local church.

Jute for freedom

When Kerry Hilton moved to India, he was stunned by the sight of 6,000 women and girls prostituting themselves on the streets of Kolkata (Calcutta). It was 2000, and Kerry had relocated from New Zealand with his wife and three children. The women lined the streets of Sonagachi, one of Asia's largest red-light districts, enticing customers. More than 2.3 million girls and women are believed to make up India's sex industry – and prostitution transactions totaled $4.1 million a day in 2004.

Although Kerry had moved to India to minister to such women, he didn't know where to begin. But he thought, 'If business could get them into the sex industry, why can't business get them out – and help them find Jesus at the same time?' A friend helped Kerry draw up a business plan. They experimented with manufacturing leather bags, buffalo-horn products, and finally jute, an environmentally friendly fiber. Locally produced cotton bags couldn't compete with China's low prices, but since India grows a majority of the world's jute, they determined that jute bags could compete.

Kerry rented a building surrounded by brothels and hired twenty women who wanted to escape prostitution. Kerry's wife, Annie, trained the women in a couple of months to sew 30 jute bags a day. Today, 107 former prostitutes work from 10 a.m. to 7 p.m. at Freeset, sewing 150,000 tote-bags and gift-bags a year. The bags are sold internationally, many to conference markets, and nearly all are custom-designed.[2] The women earn about $52 a month including benefits, more than they'd get paid sewing nearly anywhere else in Kolkata.

Kerry says he's not simply rescuing women; the women are also transforming the community. They pray daily at Freeset and meet in prayer cells each Wednesday. Local pastors frequently lead devotions. The women return home to the same place where they used to serve customers.

'We're seeking a business takeover – a freedom business takeover of the sex business,' Kerry says. 'We want markets, not donations.'

Not just feeling sorry

A similar 'freedom business' is booming in Cambodia, thanks to social entrepreneur Pierre Tami. The Swiss Christian businessman left the airline industry in 1994 to establish Hagar Cambodia, a shelter and rehabilitation center for women and children in Phnom Penh.

With the aid of professional staff and the World Bank's private sector arm, the International Finance Corporation, Pierre developed three flourishing businesses – producing soya-milk, sewing silk products, and cooking/catering – to provide employment for women and to help them support their families.

Last year, Hagar Catering donated almost half its profits to ministry. But two years ago, it was on the verge of closing. Frank Woods, a volunteer with thirty years of experience in the catering industry, turned the business around. Frank is now financially supported by a local church in Australia; he shows the women in Hagar Catering how God can help them in their daily lives as they cook and serve meals to hotel staff and garment factory workers.

Recently, Hagar Catering won a contract for the American embassy's staff cafeteria, beating other well-established businesses. 'They chose us not because they felt sorry for us [and the women], but because of our quality service,' Pierre says. While Hagar's businesses aren't meant to fully finance its services, he expects them to become fully fledged commercial ventures generating a profit margin of 5 to 15 per cent.

Rather than a missions or church planting organization, Pierre says Hagar International is a Christian agency that witnesses via acts of Christlike compassion and justice. 'We don't use these tragedies [in women's lives] to be Bible-bashers. We journey together with them, with love and compassion, to find the injustices and speak up on their behalf in very practical terms.' The agency works with local churches, which are responsible for discipling women and girls who want to grow in their faith.

'That's not just feeling sorry for "these poor women". We want to see them fully empowered, with dignity and self-esteem, and productive in society,' Pierre explains. 'We believe the gospel of the kingdom is to bring the wholeness of life into women.'

Pierre hopes to spread his ministry model to 'Hagars' who are fleeing violence, joblessness, abuse, and rape in Afghanistan, Nepal, Vietnam and beyond. 'We believe we're part of God's response to Hagar,' he says. '"Don't be afraid. God has heard your cry and the child's."'

Beyond charity

Just Food, Inc., Freeset, and Hagar International are capitalizing on a new trend in mission – helping the poor and oppressed escape their plight through business. For the last four years, Mats Tunehag has been linking churches, agencies and Christians with business skills to ministries fighting trafficking and prostitution. As the World Evangelical Alliance's and Lausanne's senior associate for Business as Mission (BAM), Mats is calling on churches worldwide to deploy gifted business-people to work where they can create lasting change. A business approach to ministry requires market analysis – examining the local market and beyond, identifying competitors, and allocating capital – which requires involving people with business experience.

Tunehag defines BAM as business with a kingdom perspective, where God transforms people and their communities spiritually, socially, and economically. 'Business is not just about getting people a job and income,' he says. 'It's a vital instrument in the transformation process.'

Mats wants to supplement the charity model. 'We're thinking that if we're going to do something, we must raise money and give it away, by providing medical help or working in a shelter or something.'

But preventing trafficking and prostitution depends on sustainable jobs and income, so business opportunities are key. 'If God has called you to business, where should you do it?' Mats says. 'Ask [yourself]: "Where could I have the most impact for the kingdom, especially for the least, the lost, and the lowliest?"'[3]

ONE STEP FURTHER

Read: Genesis 16, the story of Hagar and Ishmael.

Reflect: Hagar calls God 'the One who sees me'. Reflect on how God responds to her unjust situation. How is this like his responses in other scriptures you've read so far?

Kerry Hilton suggests that Freeset needs markets, not donations. Mats Tunehag writes that people want jobs, not hand-outs. Has this influenced your thinking about what it means to do mission among women in prostitution or mission in general?

Pray: Business as Mission encourages people to use the skills and abilities they already have to serve God and people. Ask God how he might want you, your family or your faith community to use your skills to reach the least, the lost and the lowliest.

CHAPTER 17

The Journey to New Life

I met Bevs at Samaritana's center for women in the Philippines. She told me her story in Thelma's office, while Thelma translated for me. Colorful oil paintings surrounded us, each depicting the power of God to heal the deep wounds of exploited women.[1]

Bevs' life has come full circle. Today she is married to a loving husband and has four children. During the day she helps women pick up the pieces of their lives through Samaritana, an outreach to prostituted women in Manila. Bevs accompanies them to medical check-ups for sexually transmitted diseases and pregnancy tests. She visits their families, helps obtain birth certificates, and assists with any legal cases. 'I find joy in helping others,' she says.[2]

Bevs knows from first-hand experience that these broken women need hope for change. At 17 she left her family's rural coconut farm for Manila. Despite her mother's pleas to finish high-school first, Bevs was determined to take a year off and join her older sister as a maid there. For years she had dreamed of earning piles of money in the big city. 'But when I got a hold of money, I forgot my promise to my mom that I would go back to study,' she says.[3]

'Manila was captivating, especially at night with its lights and tall buildings,' Bevs says. But her life there was hardly glamorous – the work was exhausting and the salary small. For a year she cleaned, cooked, did laundry and cared for a family with three young children for only 350 pesos a month (about 7 US dollars). 'I cried every night,' she says. So when her cousin suggested a better-paying job packing noodles at a *panciteria* (a noodle restaurant), she jumped at the chance.

Within a few days, Bevs' boss noticed her height, long black hair and slim figure. She became a waitress on the night shift, where she served beer and chatted with customers, earning commissions for each beer she sold. The tips and higher income enabled Bevs to shop for clothes, jewelry, make-up and perfume, but the money didn't satisfy her. When her boss attempted to rape her, she quit her job, and started waitressing at J&L, a cocktail lounge in a popular entertainment district.

Bevs had been living with a boyfriend and became pregnant with her first child. But the relationship ended in disappointment, and Bevs had to pay for a babysitter and earn money for groceries.

At J&L, Bevs' income was much higher. She earned a good commission on 'ladies' drinks', the beers men bought her at a higher price than their own. Despite the money, she quickly accumulated debts on shopping sprees for new clothes and Avon products. She smoked, drank nightly, dated customers after work, and slept with some.

Bevs' affair with a married man ended with the birth of her second child. Despite earlier promises, he abandoned Bevs when the baby was born. To numb the heartbreak, Bevs got drunk nightly at work and prostituted herself to customers after work hours. 'My life had no direction because I was so angry. I only felt vengeance,' she says.

Bevs got pregnant again with another man she hoped would make her happy. When he disappeared, she became *pakawala* – desperate – and quit her job. She agreed to have a neighbor adopt the baby. Unsure where to turn, she remembered Jenny from Samaritana, who'd visited her at J&L and talked about Jesus. After giving birth at a friend's house, Bevs joined Samaritana's life training program while her parents cared for her two sons.

Bevs shared an apartment with three other women participating in Samaritana's life training programs. Living in community entailed unexpected lifestyle changes. 'My wardrobe had been miniskirts, shorts, heels, sexy blouses before. Then you had to wake up early… I was used to getting up late. I also had to change my manner of speaking… Since my companions were Christians, they didn't curse. You greeted or talked to someone with respect. It was also hard to quit smoking… I hid to smoke.'

But the benefits at Samaritana outweighed the hardships. 'I learned I can relate with others, I can be a friend,' she says. Bevs completed vocational training courses in tailoring and food processing. 'I learned so many things, and my being was changed,' she says.

Bevs also participated in a Bible study. 'The Word of God was really powerful,' she says. 'I can hide from you because you're human also, but I can't hide from God. He's the one who cleanses my body, my being, and my heart.'

After graduating from Samaritana's initial one-year training, Bevs and one of the Samaritana staff visited her family on the farm. Unlike families who rejected women involved in prostitution, Bevs' parents and siblings welcomed her back.

After another six months at Samaritana, Bevs returned to live at the farm. She soon married her neighbor. Jo-jo was a former alcoholic and a new Christian who fully accepted

Bevs' past. The couple started a small business that flourished selling knick-knacks in a local market. They also joined the local Baptist church's missions team and traveled into the mountains for outreach programs. The pastor visited her home and shared the gospel with her parents.

Life wasn't free of problems. Bevs gave birth to a sickly baby, who died after his first birthday. But many people at the funeral accepted Christ and the couple's faith grew.

'I realized that aside from being saved from prostitution, I also became an instrument for my family and other people to know about God,' Bevs says.

Eventually, the couple moved to Manila together and had two more children. Bevs began helping with Samaritana's outreaches with Jo-jo's support.

Now on Tuesday nights, Bevs frequents a busy Manila street corner where prostituting women flock, offering themselves to passers-by. Last week she and Mildred, a Samaritana staff member, invited some women for a meal at Jollybee, a local fast-food restaurant. Bevs shared her story at the table as the women listened intently:

'I'm here because God told me, "I'm bringing you back to where you came from so that you can inspire others to change." I'm telling you so you know there's hope and there are people you can go to. You just have to start somewhere and make a choice. Nothing is impossible.'[4]

Life after prostitution isn't easy. Bevs was blessed to have a family who welcomed her home and a church that reached out and accepted her. Many women and men who try to rebuild their lives do not have intact or supportive families. And instead of finding a refuge and family in the church, they often face stinging rejection.

Maria was born without hands, but she was determined to survive. When she prostituted, she covered her arms with a sweater until she got a customer. Then she'd tell him, 'Well, we don't use our hands anyway.' Later she learned to cross-stitch with her knees.[5]

After joining Samaritana, Maria got involved in a local church. But when she shared her testimony with some members, word spread quickly about her past. Maria approached the choir director about singing in the choir, but he never got back to her. Others in the church ignored her.

'Church should be a safe, welcoming place, where people are embraced regardless of their journey, and met where they are on the journey,' says Jonathan Nambu, co-director of Samaritana. But when churches ask him to send a woman to share a testimony for their missions month, he usually declines. Jonathan and his wife, Thelma, hope to train more churches and volunteers, but changing people's perceptions takes time, and the recovering women don't need more rejection.

Protective boundaries

Sil Davis of Emmaus Ministries in Chicago (see Chapter 12) helps recovering men develop good boundaries. He tells them, 'Only tell people [about your background] who will support you, after you pray. If someone asks, "Are you a guy from Emmaus?" ask, "Why do you want to know?"'[6]

Sil gives the example of Jesus and his twelve disciples. Even among the disciples, he had several most trusted friends. If the guys go to a particular church, Sil tells them, 'Go sit with so-and-so,' whom he trusts.

'When I go to church with a guy, people will ask, "Is that one of your guys?" I just laugh. I don't want to answer. People want to label them "the ex-prostitute" or "the ex-gay".

How about "a child of God"? We have a hierarchy of sin within the church. It makes people feel good to help someone who's prostituted, because, "Lord, I may have sinned, but I've never prostituted."'

Reversing society's stigma

In Cambodia, 'violated women are at the bottom of the heap' in society, says Pierre Tami of Hagar International. 'This attitude is a major obstacle for reintegration' to society. Hagar created its own businesses so the women could work together and wouldn't have to face societal stigma alone.[7]

Tami compares hiking up a Swiss mountain to the women's journeys: 'When you get on top, you're heavily laden with your big burden of the past. The wounds are psychological and physical. It's a long, lonely journey.

'We want to see them reintegrated, but that's very difficult because they're so stigmatized. Even in the West, the church has a long way to go in providing acceptance – we have these walls we put up.

'The church must seek to reverse this mind-set and provide acceptance, love and a non-judgmental attitude.'

Life-long support

Edwina Gately, founder of Genesis House in Chicago, began leading country retreats for small groups of women after realizing they never had real vacations. Usually girls aged 12 to 18 join the three-day retreats, including those who have been in long-term recovery, out for four or five years, or a few who have only recently left prostitution.[8]

The retreats are a mix of group activities and time for individual counseling and rest, including fun, pampering and spiritual renewal. Gately says it's hard for most people to grasp how challenging it is for a woman with a wounded past and little self-esteem to deal with daily life. 'Prostitution demands a lifetime of recovery.'[9] The retreats and ongoing support help them stay out of prostitution.

Many of the women come from dysfunctional families, so Gately's network becomes their family. The experience of receiving love and validation helps the women to help others.[10]

Restoring a family

After Ana* (see Chapter 3) accepted Christ and joined Rahab Foundation's program for women leaving prostitution, she began talking about her healing and sharing Christ with her siblings. 'The ghost of abuse haunts them,' she says. 'I've asked God for healing so I can be an example for them. They've asked me, "How can you forgive?"'[11]

Ana married a man who encouraged her to seek healing for all the abuse of her past. But during her time in Rahab's program, he fell into adultery. She's been separated from him for eight months while he's flitted from woman to woman.

'My life has been to suffer and cry. I want to see change,' Ana says. She has seen huge changes in her family already. Ana sought reconciliation with her mother, who accepted Christ into her heart. Her younger sister, who began prostituting at age 11, joined Ana at Rahab and lives with her now. She's studying computer skills to become a secretary. Two other siblings have accepted Christ.

Ana dreams of going to Africa as a missionary and working with street children. 'God showed me I'd go to many nations and bring healing, freedom and liberation. I don't know what else, but I know it means giving kids lots of hugs.'

'Only God can make things new,' she says. 'Even if I have problems and trouble, I know I'll be victorious. I always thought only bad things could happen to me, but now I know the Good News.'

ONE STEP FURTHER

Read: Luke 7:36–50: Jesus is anointed by a sinful woman.

Reflect: The woman who poured her alabaster jar of expensive perfume over Jesus' feet sacrificed this expensive perfume as an act of gratitude and worship. Despite her sinful past and being labeled as a 'sinner', she dared to approach Jesus in the Pharisee's house to offer her valuable gift, confident of his receptivity.

How would you feel about a prostituted man or woman attending your church?

If we were all given labels based on our worst sins, what would yours be?

What resource or talent has God given you that you can pour out at Jesus' feet in service of the kingdom?

Pray: Praise God for his power and restorative work in Bevs' and Ana's lives. You might like to choose another woman or man you've read about to pray for also.

PART 3

Your Part in the Story

CHAPTER 18

Foundations for Ministry

One night in 1997, Jennifer Roemhildt, 29, an American missionary in Athens, Greece, was walking home from the refugee center where she worked. She passed through Omonia, a historic square and night-time hang-out for drug dealers and prostituted men and women. Jennifer noticed a woman on the sidewalk whose skimpy outfit and heavy make-up indicated her intent to sell her body that night.[1]

'It felt like I saw her because I was supposed to do something,' Jennifer told me. 'But I had no idea how to approach a woman in prostitution... What do I say, how do I relate to her?' After that first night, Jennifer passed this same woman three or four times. She began praying for her and other prostituted women in that neighborhood.

At an evening church service, she prayed for an opportunity to talk to the women. That same night as Jennifer walked home, she approached a hotel where a couple of women and a tall transvestite in high heels and short skirt were gathered. He stepped out and asked, 'You got the time?' Jennifer replied and continued walking home. But she couldn't get the man out of her head and couldn't stop praying for him. 'I need to go back,' she thought. 'Then I thought, that's the stupidest thing I could do. It's 11 p.m., and so on.'

Jennifer turned around, fighting with God with each step. 'You have to tell me what I'm supposed to do,' she prayed. Finally, she decided to ask the trio their names. 'I thought, most people don't know their names – they're just women on the street.'

But when she returned, only one remained – the same woman she'd passed multiple times before.

Jennifer: 'I was walking home and God told me to come back and talk to you. What's your name?'

Woman: 'It's Elise.'

The two women talked for a while before Jennifer said, 'I'm going to be praying for you.'

Elise: 'Would you pray for me now?'

'She took both my hands, and as we prayed, she said, "Yes, Lord",' says Jennifer.

Each time Jennifer passed down that street, she greeted Elise. Over the next month, Elise introduced her to five or six other women in prostitution at that hotel. 'God was building his heart for these women in me,' Jennifer says. Soon she began going out of her way to talk to the women, not just after work or church. 'Then I started talking to my friends and others who were interested, and we started praying, "God, how do you want us to respond?"'

Starting with prayer

Reaching people trapped in global prostitution and sex trafficking requires no complex formula, education or wealth. The battle over the devil's bedroom is in prayer. But the temptation is to rush to do justice in our human strength to help rescue those 'poor suffering souls'. After all, 'The only thing necessary for the triumph of evil is for good men to do nothing' (Edmund Burke). But effective change is marinated first in the action of prayer.

'We all wanted formulas, a way to do this,' Jennifer told me. But dependence on God was her first and ongoing lesson in discerning how to help. She studied Scripture with others who were praying. Together they discovered the keys for moving forward: 'We realized there's not going to be a formula; it's going to be dependence on God – listening to God for direction and then doing what he says,' she said.

Lauran Bethell, director of the International Christian Alliance on Prostitution (ICAP), emphasizes that God is the ultimate ministry designer and it's his work. While people need to learn from each other, each culture, ethnic group and economic situation needs a program specifically designed for that particular place. That way, 'It doesn't become the model for ministry from this place imposed on that place, the model from here going there,' she says.[2]

Guidelines are key

Prayer without additional support is not enough for launching an outreach. Josephine Wakeling of the National Christian Alliance on Prostitution (NCAP), a network of projects in the UK, has witnessed many projects start without necessary policies and procedures in place. 'Insufficient training and infrastructure can have considerable impact on the long-term sustainability of the project,' she says. 'It's like you are building a bridge across a chasm – you can either make it out of rope or steel, but steel is obviously going to weather the storms.'[3]

Josephine has witnessed how a project's weak foundation can take a serious toll: burn-out, allegations of abuse made against employees and volunteers, psychological breakdown of volunteers, relapse, and secondary trauma of employees. 'I have seen so many casualties among people I know,' she says.

'When we began working in the East End of London, I remember clearly God saying to me, "I can't trust you with the women yet – you are not ready,"' Josephine says. 'We had not done our bit to make the project strong enough to support people with such complex needs.'

Since NCAP began in the mid 1990s, affiliated projects have gained increasing awareness of their great responsibility toward the vulnerable women, men and children they serve. Josephine wants to ensure that projects offer high-quality support.

Although there aren't simple formulas, today there are good practice guidelines available with cross-cultural application. Based on the experiences of its forty-three affiliated projects, NCAP has developed *A Good Practice Guide*, a resource compiling years of shared learning. 'We hope it offers a consistent standard for providing care and support. We have a responsibility to love and serve with excellence,' Josephine says.

Collaboration

Prayer, preparation and commitment are essential for starting effective outreach in red-light districts or to men and women trapped elsewhere in the devil's bedroom. Awareness of existing ministries is also key.

In 2007 in London's Soho area, two different churches launched outreaches, unbeknownst to each other. Their enthusiasm had swelled following the murders of five prostituted women in Ipswich, and the churches' awakening to their responsibility to share Christ's love. Unfortunately, 'The right hand didn't know what the left hand was doing,' says Eileen,* who'd been visiting the same flats in Soho for seventeen years, befriending women in prostitution.[4]

Eileen informed the two groups of each other's work, and shortly thereafter one stopped its open-air preaching and did not return. The other is now collaborating with Eileen's church, offering refreshments and hoping to reach out to people on the streets one-on-one.

'Because this is long-term relationship work, if people come for one week, it doesn't help,' Eileen says. Trust takes time to build among the women.

Dr Beth Grant of Project Rescue also cautions, 'Don't start something by yourself.' By praying together and joining hands with others, she says, Jesus' light will shine brighter into the darkness of global sexual exploitation. 'All of us have different gifts, and it's going to take everything we have. May God help us to walk together in faith.'[5]

God's heart

Both initially and ultimately, 'The goal is that we come to have God's heart for these people and see them as God sees them,' Lauran says. And that means more than sharing the gospel with them and hoping for their salvation.

Lauran says, 'If you go out with the intention to convert, rather than to love the women, you will find it all the more difficult to cope if the women continuously reject your attempts to lead them to Christ... Make sure your motives are pure. Is it a case of conditional love – that if they do not do what you want them to do, you will eventually reject them? Or will you, like Christ himself, continue to love the woman for herself even though she does not turn to the Lord?'[6]

Lauran has led multiple groups on outings to red-light districts as a first step to understanding God's heart. For anyone who senses a call to ministry, she urges prayer. 'Go to a red-light district and park where you can see the women from a distance. Pray for them there.'

Or, 'Go to a club and park where you can see the customers coming in and out. Pray for them, pray for the women inside, the bouncers, the managers… that they would come to know God's love.'

Grasping God's love for people mired in the darkness and shunned by society entails realizing our equality as sinners. Neither women or men in prostitution, nor the Christian who tithes regularly and worships in Sunday service can do anything to save themselves.

Today volunteers and staff at Nea Zoi carry baskets stuffed with books and tracts, fliers on health and legal issues, hot drinks and cookies inside brothels and on street outreach. 'But it's not the tea, the cookies or the pamphlets… what we have to offer is God in us – that our story is part of their story,' Jennifer Roemhildt says.[7]

Beth Grant says the gospel message is the same for women around the world: 'You have value, God has a purpose for your life, and if your life is in God's hands… God can use you in ways you could never imagine.' This message of hope is identical for a 13-year-old trafficked girl, a college student, a young professional woman or a mother of three.[8]

Groups to contact

The following groups offer training, resources and advice for people interested in starting ministries or enhancing existing ones:

- **The International Christian Alliance on Prostitution (ICAP)** offers training, resources and networking opportunities to dozens of existing projects and encourages the growth of new ministries. A biennial conference gathers ministry leaders and workers from around the globe. Email: infoicap@gmail.com

- The National Christian Alliance on Prostitution (NCAP) is a collaborative network in the UK which exists to unite, equip and empower organizations seeking to offer freedom and change to those involved in prostitution. Resources for churches (the 'Sign Post Series') and the *Good Practice Guide* mentioned above are available from NCAP. Website: www.ncapuk.org   Email: ncap@ncapuk.org

---

ONE STEP FURTHER

Read: 1 Kings 19:9–12: the Lord appears to Elijah.

Reflect: God is faithful to hear our prayers and offer wisdom and direction. But he desires attentive listeners. He spoke to Elijah through a whisper. Are you open to hearing God speak to you about reaching his children who are sexually exploited?

Pray: To hear God's whispers in your life. Ask how God may want you to accompany him in reaching people trapped in the devil's bedroom.

CHAPTER 19

Investing Your Talents

Jamelyn told me about her time in Costa Rica one Saturday morning at my dining-room table. I'd met her a few months earlier when she spoke at her home church about volunteering with Rahab Foundation in Costa Rica.[1]

'I remember leaving US soil at Miami, gripping the airplane seats and thinking, "Oh my goodness, what have I gotten myself into?" That moment there was nothing but God. I knew that if God wanted me there, he was going to give me the skills.'

Jamelyn Lederhouse spent a year with Rahab Foundation in Costa Rica one year after graduating from college with an education degree. Her Spanish wasn't fluent and she'd never been involved with prostituting women or girls at risk, but she wanted an opportunity to serve and boost her Spanish skills. 'I wanted to give back for all that I have received,' she says. 'It wasn't like I woke up one day and said, "I want to work with prostitutes." It's not like I, the little white girl from DuPage County, had a lot of life experience to share.'

But Jamelyn was willing to go and learn. From January to November 2006, she led an after-school program for girls aged 12 to 18 who were at risk or involved in prostitution. Their mothers were often participants in Rahab's recovery and training program for women wanting to leave prostitution.

The small group of six to eight girls bonded over movies, hiking, drama and discussions about boyfriends, love and God.

One of the girls, Naomi, 16, had dropped out of school after 3rd grade and came from a destitute family. She had only three shirts, one of which barely held together with one button and a safety pin. The staff suspected she might be involved in prostitution. When Jamelyn first met Naomi, she seemed shy and fragile, and was always first to leave. Jamelyn made sure to say hi and ask about her day, conveying acceptance and respect. Over the year, Naomi warmed to her, and Jamelyn witnessed a dramatic change in her growth and confidence.

For one activity, the girls developed, produced and starred in a play. They aimed to enable their mothers to walk in their daughters' shoes. The scenes included a mother too busy working to be present for her children, a father who abuses the children, and a daughter who's failing in school, smoking and cutting classes with the wrong crowd. When two friends invite the girl to church, she learns how Jesus has power to help and heal her family. Besides bonding together, creating and performing the play boosted the girls' confidence and helped them realize they had a story to tell.

Jamelyn learned that any discussion about God needed to be very practical. 'Because the girls didn't have good father figures, God as their father figure was a hard, abstract concept for them to grasp,' she says. Instead she emphasized Christ, a source of strength they could call on for personal help.

She gained from the same lesson. 'I learned a lot when I felt lost and ineffective,' she says. 'It was a big thing to go from saying, "No, I can't do that" to "Yes, I can," but knowing where my strength comes from.'

Prostitution and trafficking ministries require huge investments to help restore individual lives, so volunteers are critical.

'You're adopting people – that takes a lot of money, time and resources,' Jamelyn says. 'It's a costly ministry, so it needs a lot of support and help in all facets. Everyone can make a difference, if they actively choose to.'

Many groups seek short-term teams from churches, early retirees who can offer long-term help, or people willing to volunteer from their own home. Just Food, Inc. in Thailand has a wish-list for congregations: computer people, nurses, construction people, electricians, business people... and the list continues. They also need people willing to help with their website from abroad.[2]

Local volunteer mentors are invaluable for many ministries. The Scarlet Cord in Amsterdam seeks Christian women for its 'Buddy Program'. Every woman who decides to leave prostitution is asked if she wants to be paired with a 'buddy', a woman to meet with her every two weeks for coffee and conversation. Buddies must have three friends who are praying for the woman. The aim is a consistent, supportive friend and Christian witness. Currently nine pairs of women are meeting, but two women are still waiting for a 'buddy' to volunteer.[3]

Room for guys?

Women are not the only volunteers that ministries seek. When Thelma Nambu first asked her husband, Jonathan, to work with Samaritana, he hesitated. As a male, he couldn't see a clear role for himself in a ministry to women recovering from exploitation by men. But Jonathan agreed to work behind the scenes in administration and management.[4]

When Bevs (see Chapter 17) told Jonathan that thanks to him, she realized not all men were bad, he changed his mind.

'I've come to believe a male presence is helpful for the women. It's part of their healing journey to relate in non-sexual ways with men,' he told me. 'There will always be a role for men within boundaries, and a role that women can't play.'

At the Salvation Army's Faith House in London's King Cross (see Chapter 14), a majority of volunteers are Christian men. Clear ground-rules for both men and women help create a safe environment for both volunteers and visitors from the streets. After an initial background check, manager Estelle Blake observes men who volunteer for their first month or two. The main rules are: a man will not have any physical contact with women; he'll never be alone with the women; and he'll say a code word if he feels unsafe or uncomfortable.[5]

'Some men can't hack it because some of the women are quite flirtatious,' Estelle says. 'It's as much making sure the men are safe as the women [we're working with] are safe.'

The men go on street outreach, paired with a woman volunteer, and come on Wednesday nights for dinner and fellowship with men and women from the streets. 'The guys have been brilliant for a lot of the women because they've established safe relationships with them,' Estelle says.

'They're safe men, men who don't want anything from them. It's helped the women understand what's right and what's okay in a relationship with a man.'

One male volunteer sat in a chair every Wednesday night for eighteen months and never initiated conversation. The women approached him. As soon as he got to know them, he'd stand up and shake their hand. Over time, the women realized that they could trust him and that he didn't want anything sexual from them. The volunteer in turn realized that 'evangelism is about sitting' as much as proclaiming the gospel.

'Show them my heart'

I met Eileen* at a Starbucks near London's Piccadilly Square. Over tea she told me about what she's learned from years of ministry, then took me on a walking tour of Soho's back streets. She pointed out the scribbled signs tacked beside doorways that read 'Model Upstairs' – code for 'prostituted woman here'.[6]

Eileen has been knocking on the same brothel doors in London's fashionable Soho district for the last seventeen years. The Swiss missionary visits sixty flats at least once a month each, introducing herself to new women, and offering practical and emotional help, and prayer on her second or third visits. As they begin to trust her, she forms friendships with the women and with the maids who work in the flats.

Perseverance and obedience to God's call to reach these women is key, because visible results are few. 'You have to be aware you're there for God, sometimes only [in their lives] for a short season, to plant the seeds and somebody else will water them,' says Eileen.

'I've asked God if there's another way to produce quicker salvation and results,' she says. Each time she asks, God shows her a picture of two hands holding a big heart. '"Show them my heart," he says.'

Trying the three Ts

At Emmaus Ministries in Chicago, I learned that presence is powerful for men who've been abandoned repeatedly. Last autumn, my husband, his former room-mate, a girlfriend and I cooked up pots of chilli and pans of cornbread for Saturday-night dinner at the Emmaus drop-in center. Besides the meal,

I wasn't sure what we suburbanites would be offering to men whom I imagined had been hardened by years of tough street life. But I had committed to writing a magazine article about Emmaus and I wanted to do more than just interview people from the distant role of reporter.

'The three Ts are time, touch and talk,' director John Green told us when we arrived. 'Shake a guy's hand, slap him on the back, and spend time talking and listening. If you're able to offer these to the men, you'll be doing a great service.'

Eating together and hanging out afterward was less awkward than I'd anticipated. Dinner conversation included the latest movie releases and was interrupted by requests to pass the salad dressing or cornbread. After the guys had finished washing the dishes, some were eager to talk. Henry,* a freckled red-head, sat quietly on a couch at first. But when I asked him where he was from, he slowly began opening up about his family life in Appalachia and his love for car racing on isolated country roads at night.

I interpreted for another woman as she prayed aloud in Spanish with Andy (Chapter 4), that he would know God's power in his life. Teary-eyed, he gave us both hugs. I started to grasp that the three Ts speak volumes to the men, who may begin to believe you're there because you care.

There are umpteen opportunities to use your professional skills and natural gifts to help a ministry, whether you have talents in business, drama, finance, cooking, sewing, marketing, computers, teaching or you name it.

Advocacy

Dr Beth Grant is co-founder of Project Rescue, a ministry of Assemblies of God World Missions and national churches. I talked with this woman of powerful convictions in LA after she spoke at a sex trafficking conference.[7]

'Last year when I was in a home [for girls and women] in Calcutta, they asked me to do a devotional at the last minute. I'm sitting with a group of young women at a vocational training center. Half of them had just walked out of brothels and come to learn a new trade. For several, it was the first time they'd ever come. They walk in and sit down, and I'm sharing a devotional. I thought, "Oh God, here I am, my life and [privileged] background. How can I connect?"

'I thought about Esther's life and how many things she had absolutely no control over. She was orphaned, taken to a foreign country, taken into the harem – a treacherous place. All these things separated her from family and culture. She had no control, but God had his hand on her life and had a purpose. I talked about how God gave Esther a platform. When the time came, she was ready to speak, and her words saved her people.

'I felt so strongly for those women in that training center, walking out of the red-light district. I believe one day they will be the ones to have a platform and speak about this issue, not me. They are becoming new women. I believe God will give them the platform… We are helping empower and bring healing… but in the future, they will be the ones who stand up and say, "This atrocity needs to stop. And for those who have already been exploited, there is hope." For them to say it, has real meaning.'

God needs both local Esthers and modern-day prophets to speak out against injustice in our homes, communities, churches, cities, countries and beyond national borders. We have multiple opportunities to reveal the enemy's lies about sexuality in our own societies and begin replacing them with truths. Here are just a few examples of how you can advocate for societies free of sexual exploitation.

Porn and pancakes

Address the pervasiveness of porn and the victims it creates – both the consumers and the people posing – by starting with your own church. Imagine talking about porn addictions over coffee and a stack of cakes dripping with syrup, in your church fellowship hall. I hope we all have the opportunity someday.

The power of porn grows in the darkness. It's the dirty little secret that your and my cousin, friend or spouse keeps. But it's also the start of sexual addictions that ultimately feed prostitution and sex trafficking.

Churches can tackle this topic head-on and bring it into the light, initiating the journey of healing by creating a safe forum for discussion. The breakfast is open to men and boys from junior high school and upwards. XXXChurch.com is seeking churches around the US willing to host this event. Visit www.pornandpancakes.com

Not for Sale Sunday

Join with churches across the UK to raise awareness of women, children and men subject to sexual exploitation. Rally your church and community together on the designated day for 'Not for Sale Sunday' and affirm that these women and children and men are made in the image of God. Resources such as Bible studies, music, readings, liturgies and publicity materials are available from CHASTE (Churches Alert to Sex Trafficking Across Europe). Visit www.chaste.org.uk (email: notforsalesunday@chaste.org.uk and contact@notforsaleuk.org).

International Weekend of Fasting and Prayer for Victims of Human Trafficking

Pray and fast annually with Christians around the globe on a designated weekend as God calls and guides his people on behalf of those who are deceived, enslaved, victimized and brutalized. The Salvation Army offers online resources for prayer, sermons, Bible studies, fliers and more. Available at www.salvationarmyusa.org

House events

House events offer a cosy and welcoming environment for friends, neighbors and church members to learn about God's work in a specific ministry. For example, Emmaus Ministries in Chicago offers 'Stories on the Streets', a compelling combination of music, story-telling and dramatic monologue that tells the stories of men on the streets, presented by singers and songwriters, Andy and Al Tauber.

Grassroots ministries around the globe rely on the prayer, involvement and support of individual Christians to carry out their work. They often seek to raise awareness and support for projects around the globe. Does your church already have a specific geographical area it supports in missions? Find out what grassroots ministries are located in that area and invite a speaker into your home. If they can't send someone, offer to raise awareness yourself. They may be able to send you brochures, DVDs or other information. Contact ICAP to find a grassroots ministry: infoicap@gmail.com

Power in numbers: Denominational advocacy

The power of the church to influence local communities and create ripples of change around the world is undeniable. When entire denominations collaborate in a cause, the impact is exponentially greater.

The Baptist Union of Sweden

The Baptist Union of Sweden has been coordinating the European Baptist Federation's work against human trafficking, encompassing 13,000 congregations in 54 countries.[8] Since 2005, the Baptist Union of Sweden has been a member of a unique partnership among government, police, universities, a museum, independent groups and churches. The partnership 'Samverkan mot trafficking' ('cooperation against trafficking') aims to raise public awareness, develop a network of support for trafficking victims, and streamline legal procedures against perpetrators. Action items include: a trafficking hotline, safe houses for victims, and a museum exhibition on trafficking.

Project Rescue

Project Rescue is a ministry of Assemblies of God World Missions and national churches that began when Bombay Teen Challenge ministers inspired more than 100 young women to escape the chains of prostitution and find new life in Christ. They sought church partners to help provide safe homes for the women leaving brothels and for the daughters of prostituted women who hoped to protect their daughters from exploitation. The partnership between Assemblies of God and Bombay Teen Challenge resulted in a Home of Hope, a safe house where the women and young girls can live in a nurturing environment. Today Project Rescue offers eleven places of refuge in nine cities of South Asia and plans to expand to Moldova, Ukraine and Russia.[9]

Each site is connected with at least one local church from the beginning. The church offers a supportive community, possible funding help, staff, volunteers to lead devotions and more. 'The church must offer a genuine community for the girls, or they won't survive – they'll go back,' says Dr Beth

Grant, Project Rescue co-founder. 'At least they had relationships in the brothels.'[10]

Internationally the homes are supported by individuals, churches, and women's ministries of Assemblies of God churches who raise funds and prayer support for starting new homes. Project Rescue also encourages small groups – students in dorms, women's groups, or others – to raise awareness, pray and connect with the Homes of Hope.[11]

ONE STEP FURTHER

Read: Matthew 25:14–30: the Parable of the Talents.

Reflect: This parable reveals that those who claim to be Jesus' followers but do not invest in the kingdom will be held accountable. We have the opportunity to multiply what God has entrusted to us. What gifts has God entrusted you with? Are you being a good steward of those gifts?

Pray: Commit your gifts to the Lord. Ask if he'd like you to use any for building his kingdom among survivors of prostitution or trafficking.

Chapter 20

Building the Body

The Well is a support house for women exiting the sex industry or at risk of becoming involved (see Chapter 15). Kelly writes about her experience with church:

> I have always had good experiences with people at the church. The church to me has always been a place of peace and comfort and an escape from the disruptive home life I was living.
>
> I first started to go to church when my children were small. I was heavily into drugs, just started as a sex worker and living with my partner, who was also my children's dad and… using drugs.
>
> I don't know why, but I was walking home from the shops one day and just felt the urge to walk into church. I was very much welcomed by the people inside, and they told me to come along to the Sunday service. I did, and as I started to sing along to the hymns I was suddenly overwhelmed with tears, but they weren't tears of sadness, they were tears of a belonging and peace and comfort. I've been going to church ever since.
>
> I feel even though I've been a drug addict and sex worker I am still accepted into the church, which is very

important. I feel the churches I have been to have made me feel no different at all, and have made me feel equal to everyone else.[1]

Not all people are called to get directly involved in a ministry to men and women wounded by sexual exploitation. But we are all called to be and to build our local Body of Christ. Churches worldwide have potential to become safe places of acceptance, friendship, healing and restoration, offering Christian community that transforms lives.

Belonging to a caring community is a universal desire, says Jonathan Nambu of Samaritana in the Philippines. 'Ultimately, what the women [and men coming out of prostitution] long for, like all of us, is to be in a place where we feel safe and respected, welcome and embraced even as our stories are also known.[2] 7

'The women [and men] need to feel a part of something larger, but I believe that in many ways they also yearn for a sense of deep community that is often elusive in large sanctuaries, worship halls, and cathedrals.'

Inside the larger church body, smaller groups of Christian community such as cell groups, families, or other groups, are integral for providing relationships of intimacy, trust and caring. These groups need to be more than an exclusive, inward-focused clique, Jonathan says.

'High levels of intimacy coupled with a high commitment to mission and outreach, especially to the vulnerable and marginalized, are ideal qualities for churches who want to embrace people leaving prostitution,' he says.

Harmony Dust, founder of Treasures (see Chapters 2 and 10), left the stripping industry only after participating in a church community that welcomed her and facilitated herspiritual growth. She speaks at other churches, encouraging them to consider whether they are places of grace. 'The way the church can help is to be a place where people can come – the kind of place where any person who needs healing and restoration can come free of judgment.'[3]

Harmony describes her healing as a journey that took place within a local Body of Christ. 'You're transformed by the renewing of your mind, replacing the lies that you've been taught about yourself.' That process takes time, plus the prayers and presence of God's people. 'We have to love people and give them grace as they go through that process,' she says.

When people ask Harmony for advice about starting an outreach to local strip-clubs, she first asks whether their own church and pastors are supportive. 'If we go out with love, smiles and grace and invite them to a place where they're not going to experience that, then what's the point?'

Church leaders must model Christ's unconditional love in order to create a welcoming atmosphere and community for broken people, says Alex Jones-Moreno, missions pastor of Harmony's church, The Oasis Center. 'In everything that we do… these are the values we communicate – you'll be welcome, feel comfortable and safe. We're going to do our best to not judge you and to be available for you,' he says. 'We leave space for the Holy Spirit to work.'[4]

Alex and other church leaders often share their own stories of brokenness, so people at Oasis know they're not alone. He openly describes his near-failed marriage, his sexual abuse experience and other hardships before he found healing and restoration. 'We are all incredibly imperfect people called to do God's work,' he says.

The stigma at church

Betsy* invited Emily,* a woman who worked on the streets, to visit her church. They entered the church, but Emily stopped at the back, where she gazed at the people gathering for the service. After a few minutes, she backed out of the building. 'What's wrong?' Betsy asked.

'I already know way too many people in there,' Emily said. She recognized men in the church who had 'purchased' sex from her. If she went in, how would she be treated? Would the church support her, the woman in racy clothes? Or would they side with the men inside the doors whose children sat in Sunday school? The potential stigma was too hard for Emily to bear.[5]

The paradox of the church, Jesus' witness this side of heaven, is its people – the greatest sinners on earth. When we grasp and accept our own stories of brokenness, we can welcome others with a full embrace instead of judging them from a distance. Or, we can separate ourselves from those living outside our 'pure white walls' in sexual sin, and add to the rejection and stigma they already endure.

Ultimately, the end goal is the same for every person who accepts Christ's invitation to drink from the well of living waters. After welcoming us into his Father's kingdom, Jesus calls us to become his disciples and use our gifts to bless others.

To the church he has entrusted the keys of the kingdom, and he has appointed us to be ambassadors to the earth's darkest corners, whether across town or overseas. Jesus is already there, waiting to introduce us to the men, women and children whom he loves. Will we respond to his invitation and follow wherever he leads?

ONE STEP FURTHER

Read: John 8:2–11: the adulterous woman who is about to be stoned to death.

Reflect: Jesus exposed the depth of society's hypocrisy and our habits of casting guilt and blame. Sin has permeated human nature, not just the man or woman involved in sexual sin. Do we welcome people of all backgrounds in our churches and help lead them to Christ? Or must they first conform to our standards of appearance and behavior? What can you do to help create an atmosphere of welcome in your faith community?

Pray:

Lord, open our eyes,
That we may see you in our brothers and sisters.
Lord, open our ears,
That we may hear the cries of the hungry, the cold, the
frightened, the oppressed.
Lord, open our hearts,
That we may love each other as you love us.
Renew in us your Spirit.
Lord, free us and make us one.

Mother Teresa of Calcutta

CHAPTER 21

Open Our Eyes

During the two years that I spent procrastinating, pondering, praying and researching for this book, I talked with friends over dinner, trail-walks and long-distance phone calls. Many had heard about the problems of sex trafficking and prostitution via news reports. They always congratulated me on my writing endeavor, but our conversations often concluded with the same comments: 'It's such an awful problem, but what can we do?'

Our heartstrings are pulled, but we shrug our shoulders because, in all honesty, this global problem is utterly daunting. The massive injustice of commercial sexual exploitation screams for intervention from God's people. Will you look away, overwhelmed by the sheer evil and stench of darkness? Or will you pray for eyes of compassion and ask God to use you in this battle? The cost of following Christ is not cheap. And if we do not prioritize, we can easily lose ourselves in the busyness of books to study, a pending work project, bills to pay, laundry piles, diapers to change, or parties to plan.

If God has answered my prayers, you want to make a difference and you realize that Jesus' authority is greater than the darkest powers. You have heard God whispering in your heart to *do something*.

Creating change through prayer

So, where do we begin? Without prayer, we enter a spiritual battle with human equipment, insufficient for breaking the thick chains in the devil's bedroom. Prayer is our mysterious resource. This gift allows us to co-labor with God to create eternal change in the universe. Ironically, prayer is not dependent on human strength. Through our prayers, God channels his power through the Holy Spirit.

Even better than our solitary prayers, when two or three believers are gathered in Jesus' name, interceding for others, God promises to act. So, grab a friend or family member, or enlist your small group or Bible study to pray regularly about this topic. Pick a ministry to pray for and get on their mailing list. Or rotate prayer for ministries in different locations. My sweetest times in writing this book have been praying with friends for the men and women on these pages.

There is no shortage of specific ways in which you can intercede and change lives from half-way around the world or in your own city.

The following basic guidelines are included in the Salvation Army's 'Prayer Guide for the International Weekend of Prayer & Fasting for Victims of Sex Trafficking'. More detailed prayer suggestions are available in the actual prayer guide.[1]

- Restoration: Pray for the rescue and restoration of the countless number of people who have become victims of sexual trafficking and commercial exploitation.
- Breakdown of the sex industry: Pray for the demise of the sex industry – porn, strip-clubs, lap-dancing clubs, brothels – and for strong law enforcement.
- Decreased demand: Pray for efforts that reduce demand for commercial sex, including defeating attempts to legalize

prostitution or repealing legalization in various countries. Pray for programs and ministries that help men and women with sexual addictions.

- **Development:** Pray for the economic and social development of poverty-stricken nations, to eradicate the conditions that facilitate sexual exploitation.
- **World leaders:** Pray that people in positions of power and influence allocate the time and resources necessary to confronting sexual exploitation.
- **The church:** Pray for an increase of resources – human, financial and spiritual – to meet the needs of survivors; for collaboration among Christian groups; and for vision, strength and leadership among Christians working on this issue.

Consider going through the Salvation Army's Bible study lessons for examining God's heart and our role in reaching men, women and children who are sexually exploited.[2]

Giving

Resources are critical for prostitution and trafficking ministries that require huge investments in individual lives. Many ministries struggle to cover the day-to-day costs of renting an office, covering often low staff salaries, or paying for the gifts, books or snacks offered to exploited people. To fill the gap, some ministries receive government funding and then are restricted in how they use the resources.

If you value the impact of ministries at work in the devil's bedroom, back your prayers with your bank account and choose one or several to which you will contribute regularly. Invite your small group or church to join you and share the blessing of giving. Hold a fund-raiser for a specific project and help spread the word about God's work among exploited men and women.

If you like to know exactly what you're funding, many ministries have specific needs – whether building a new home for trafficked girls or purchasing a van for outreach events. My own church raised thousands of dollars on Good Friday to help construct a ministry's new building. In some cases, you may be able to donate the specific item(s) needed, such as computers, furniture or gifts for special holiday outreaches.

Too late?

The devil's bedroom is crammed with people – the porn users, the corrupt police officers, the brothel owners, not to mention the men, women and children whose bodies are bought and sold as daily commodities. On a human level, this fortress of evil is too strong for one person or even one church.

Our challenge today is believing that God's power through the global church is greater than the devil's bondage. Kingdom principles are the same yesterday, today and tomorrow, as in Jesus' meeting with Jairus.[3]

Amidst the swelling crowds seeking Jesus 2,000 years ago, Jairus, a desperate father, threw himself at Jesus' feet, begging for help. This synagogue ruler's only daughter, just 12 years old, was deathly ill. Jairus begged for his daughter's life from his humbled position on the ground. Would Jesus come quickly? Of course. But the crowds jostled and clamored for Jesus' attention as he walked with Jairus.

Before they reached the house, servants sent word of the girl's death. 'Don't be afraid – just believe, and she will be healed,' Jesus told Jairus. The grieving father had a choice. Would he believe Jesus or the physical facts that his servants reported?

They finally reached the house, where Jesus commanded all the mourners, 'Stop wailing! She is not dead, but asleep.'

They too could choose to believe Jesus or what they saw with their eyes. They laughed in his face. Who was he to say she wasn't dead? They had witnessed the girl's life slip away moments earlier.

But Jesus clasped the girl's hand, and said, 'My child, get up!' And she did.

Confronted by human disbelief and a physically impossible task, Jesus healed the dead girl and gave her new life. He offers the same gift of new life to people struggling with sexual addictions, brothel owners, transgendered people, prostituted men and women, and children suffering from abuse. But he also asks us the same question: will we believe in his power to heal beyond the grips of death? By all appearances, these people are dead – too wounded for hope and too depraved to be healed.

Our response now is more critical than when Jesus walked the dusty roads on earth. Today we are his eyes for hoping, his heart for loving, his hands of healing, and his feet for approaching those sitting in darkness. If we don't believe in his power, how will they escape the devil's bedroom? How will they discover the freedom and fullness of a new life?

Resources

CHASTE: Churches Alert to Sex Trafficking Across Europe (www.chaste.org.uk) is a network of churches advocating an end to sex trafficking. CHASTE offers multiple resources for churches to raise awareness and get involved. See also: www.notforsalesunday.org.uk.

CENA: Comunidade Evangélica Nova Aurora (www.missao-cena.com.br/asp/default.asp) is an outreach to homeless people and prostituted men and women in São Paolo, Brazil.

Emmaus Ministries (www.streets.org) is an evangelical Catholic–Protestant outreach that incarnates Christ's love to prostituted men in Chicago and Houston.

Freeset (www.freesetbags.com) is a business that employs formerly prostituted women to manufacture jute bags in Calcutta, India.

GatheredVoices.com is a website that compiles writings, stories and images created primarily by people who have been exploited through prostitution or sex trafficking.

Hagar International (www.hagarproject.org) intervenes in the lives of vulnerable mothers and children by offering prevention, rehabilitation and reintegration programs.

International Association of Healing Rooms (www.healingrooms.com) is a ministry in churches and cities around the world with a common vision to bring healing back into the Body of Christ.

International Christian Alliance on Prostitution (ICAP) offers training, resources and networking opportunities to dozens of existing projects and encourages the growth of new ministries. A biennial conference gathers ministry leaders and workers from around the globe. Sign up for the prayer network to receive prayer requests from organizations. Email: infoicap@gmail.com

International Justice Mission (IJM) (www.ijm.org) is a human rights agency that rescues victims of violence, sexual exploitation, slavery and oppression.

Just Food, Inc. (www.justfoodinc.org) and the Garden of Hope reach women, children and youth involved in, at risk of, or affected by prostitution, sexual exploitation and/or trafficking in Chiang Mai and northern Thailand.

National Christian Alliance on Prostitution (NCAP) (www.ncapuk.org) is a collaborative network in the UK which exists to unite, equip and empower organizations seeking to offer freedom and change to those involved in prostitution. Resources for churches (the 'Sign Post Series') and the Good Practice Guide mentioned above are available from NCAP. Email: ncap@ncapuk.org

Nea Zoi or 'Lost Coin' (www.iteams.org) is a ministry of International Teams reaching prostituted men and women and trafficked women in Athens, Greece.

Porn and Pancakes (www.pornandpancakes.com): XXXChurch.com is seeking churches around the US willing to host this event and help start open discussion about porn. The breakfast is open to men and boys of junior high school age and upwards.

Project Rescue (www.projectrescue.org) is a ministry of Assemblies of God World Missions and national churches. Today Project Rescue offers eleven places of refuge for prostituted women and girls at risk in nine cities of South Asia.

Rahab Foundation (www.rahabfoundation.org) is a ministry to prostituted women and girls at risk in Costa Rica.

Salvation Army (www.salvationarmyusa.org) offers multiple online resources, articles and suggestions for how to get involved in ministry. See also the Initiative Against Sex Trafficking (www.iast.net).

Samaritana (www.samaritana.org) is a ministry to prostituted women in the Philippines.

Scarlet Cord (Scharlaken Koord) (http://www.tothe ildesvolks.nl/cms/content/view/40/34/) is a ministry to prostituted and trafficked women in the Netherlands. The Scarlet Cord also runs a prevention program, 'Loverboys', among teenage girls in high schools across the country.

Treasures (www.iamatreasure.com) is an outreach to women in the stripping industry based in Los Angeles, California.

World Vision (www.worldvision.org) has a child sex tourism prevention program in multiple countries.

Notes

Glossary

1. *Hands that Heal: International Curriculum to Train Caregivers of Trafficking Survivors* (draft) (Faith Alliance Against Slavery & Trafficking, 2007), p. 8.
2. 'Pimp', available from http://en.wikipedia.org/wiki/Pimp, 20 January 2008.
3. *Hands that Heal*, op. cit., p. 10.
4. National Christian Alliance on Prostitution, *A Good Practice Guide* (draft, 2007), available soon from www.ncapuk.org.
5. Ibid.
6. US Victims of Trafficking and Violence Protection Act of 2000, H.R. 3244, 106th Congress, Sec. 103.9.
7. *Hands that Heal*, op. cit., p. 9.
8. National Christian Alliance on Prostitution, *A Good Practice Guide*, op. cit.
9. Email to the author from John Green, 10 September 2007.
10. Ibid.
11. Ibid.
12. 'Trick', available from http://en.wiktionary.org/wiki/trick, 20 January 2008.

Chapter 1

1. Dawn Herzog Jewell, 'Red-Light Rescue', *Christianity Today*, January 2007, p. 30.
2. Ibid., p. 29.
3. Ibid., p. 30.
4. Ibid.
5. Ibid.
6. Ibid.

7. Melissa Farley and others, 'Prostitution and Trafficking in Nine Countries: An Update on Violence and Posttraumatic Stress Disorder', in *Prostitution, Trafficking and Traumatic Stress*, ed. Melissa Farley (Binghampton, New York: The Haworth Maltreatment & Trauma Press, 2003), p. 56.
8. Mark Crawford, telephone interview by the author, 11 May 2006.
9. John Green, email interview by the author, 19 September 2007.

Chapter 2

1. Harmony Dust, interview by Dean Curry, Life Center, Tacoma, WA, USA, 11 March 2007; available from http://www.life-center.org/podcasts/audio/070311.mp3.
2. Sheila Weller, 'No one Should Have to Be a Stripper', *Glamour*, January 2007, p. 168.
3. Ibid.
4. Ibid.
5. Harmony Dust, telephone interview by the author, 22 March 2007.
6. Treasures brochure.
7. Ibid.
8. Weller, op. cit., p. 168.
9. Ibid.
10. Ibid.
11. Ibid., p. 169.
12. Ibid.
13. Harmony Dust, interview by Dean Curry.
14. Melissa Farley and others, 'Prostitution and Trafficking in Nine Countries: An Update on Violence and Posttraumatic Stress Disorder', in *Prostitution, Trafficking and Traumatic Stress*, ed. Melissa Farley (Binghampton, New York: The Haworth Maltreatment & Trauma Press, 2003), p. 34.
15. Jody Miller and Dheeshana Jayasundara, 'Prostitution, the Sex Industry, and Sex Tourism', in *Sourcebook on Violence against Women*, eds. C.

Renzetti, J. Edleson and R. Bergen (Thousand Oaks, Calif.: Sage, 2001), p. 465, cited in *Listening to Olivia: Violence, Poverty and Prostitution*, Jody Raphael (Boston: Northeastern University Press, 2004), p. 62.

16. Stripclublist.com, cited in Jody Raphael, *Listening to Olivia*, op. cit., pp. 70–72.
17. Farley and others, op. cit., p. 63.
18. Julie Bindel, 'Profitable Exploits: Lap Dancing in the UK' (2004), in Signpost Series 3a, *Prostitution and Sex Trafficking* (National Christian Alliance on Prostitution, 1), available from http://www.nca-puk.org/documents/signpost3d.pdf.
19. Hannah Macsween, 'Prostitution: which stance to take?' (CARE for Europe AISBL, 2007), available from http://www.care.org.uk/Publisher/File.aspx?ID=126 49.
20. Harmony Dust, telephone interview.
21. Treasures brochure.
22. Sara Ann Friedman, 'Who Is There to Help Us? How the System Fails Sexually Exploited Girls in the United States' (ECPAT-USA, Inc., 2005, 4), available online at www.ecpatusa.org/documents/WhoIsTheretoHelpUS .pdf.
23. K. Holsopple, 'Strip Clubs According to Strippers: Exposing Workplace Sexual Violence' (unpublished paper, 1998), available online at http://www.catwin-ternational.org/stripc1.html, cited in Farley and others, op. cit., p. 61.
24. Jody Raphael and Deborah L. Shapiro, 'Sisters Speak Out: The Lives and Needs of Prostituted Women in Chicago: A Research Study' (report, Chicago, 2002), available at www.impactresearch.org on 29 May 2003, cited in Jody Raphael, *Listening to Olivia*, op. cit., p. 82.
25. Harmony Dust, interview by Dean Curry.
26. Ibid.
27. Farley and others, op. cit., p. 58.
28. Raphael, *Listening to Olivia*, op. cit., p. 5.

29. Raphael and Shapiro, op. cit., p. 23, cited in Jody Raphael, *Listening to Olivia*, op. cit., p. 86.
30. Eleanor Maticka-Tyndale and others, 'Exotic Dancing and Health', *Women & Health* 31, no. 1 (2000), pp. 101–2, cited in Jody Raphael, *Listening to Olivia*, op. cit., p. 87.
31. Emmily Bristol, 'Sluts Are People Too', *Las Vegas City Life*, 20 July 2006, available from http://www.lasvegascitylife.
com/articles/2006/07/20/local_news/news01.prt.
32. Emmily Bristol, 'Hot and Bothered', *Las Vegas City Life*, 15 February 2007, available from http://www.lasvegascitylife.com/articles/2007/02/15/news/cover/iq_12554578.txt.
33. Ibid.
34. Ibid.
35. Harmony Dust, interview by the author.
36. Ibid.

Chapter 3

1. Ana,* interview by the author, Green Lake, WI, USA, 22 April 2006.
2. Melissa Farley and others, 'Prostitution and Trafficking in Nine Countries: An Update on Violence and Posttraumatic Stress Disorder', in *Prostitution, Trafficking and Traumatic Stress*, ed. Melissa Farley (Binghampton, New York: The Haworth Maltreatment & Trauma Press, 2003), p. 57.
3. Ibid.
4. Ibid.
5. D. S. Morse, A. L. Suchman and R. M. Frankel, 'The Meaning of Symptoms in 10 Women with Somatization Disorder and a History of Childhood Abuse', *The Archives of Family Medicine* 6 (1997), pp. 468–76, cited in Farley and others, op. cit., p. 57.
6. Melissa Farley, ed., *Prostitution, Trafficking and Traumatic Stress* (Binghampton, New York: The Haworth Maltreatment & Trauma Press, 2003), p. 173.
7. US Department of State, *Trafficking in Persons Report*, June 2005, p. 8.

8. Ibid.

9. Libertad Latina, http://www.libertadlatina.org/Crisis_Latin _America_Introduction.htm.

10. Glenn Garvin, 'Child Sex: A Sordid Trade Booms in Costa Rica', *Miami Herald*, 1 March 2000, on the Protection Project website, http://www.protection-project.org/costa.htm.

11. Women and the Economy, a project of the United Nations Platform for Action Committee, available from http://www.unpac.ca/economy/wompov-erty2.html.

12. Libertad Latina, op. cit.

13. Dawn Herzog Jewell, 'Child Sex Tours', *Christianity Today*, January 2007, p. 32.

14. Ibid.

15. 'Summary of Statistics on Child Prostitution and Trafficking' (ECPAT-USA, April 1999), on the Protection Project website, http://www.protection-project.org/costa.htm.

16. Joseph Contreras, 'The Dark Tourists', *Newsweek International*, 2 May 2001, on the Protection Project website, http://www.protectionproject.org/costa.htm.

17. '"Sex-pats" Sexually Exploiting Poor Costa Rican Girls: ECPAT', *Agence France Presse*, 30 August 1996 on the Protection Project website, http://www.pro-tectionproject. org/costa.htm.

18. Serge F. Kovaleski, 'The Dark Side of the Tourism Industry', *Toronto Star*, 9 January 2000 on the Protection Project website, http://www.protection-project.org/costa.htm.

19. Glenn Garvin, op. cit.

20. Shelley Rice, email interview by author, 20 September 2007.

21. US Department of State, *Trafficking in Persons Report*, 2007, available online at http://sanjose.usembassy.gov/tip costarica.html.

22. Dawn Herzog Jewell, 'Child Sex Tours', op. cit.

23. Ibid.
24. Ibid.
25. Ibid.
26. Ibid.
27. Samaritana,
    http://www.samaritana.org/frameset.html?
    index.html&2.

Chapter 4

1. Andy,* telephone interview by the author, 13 October 2006.
2. Dawn Herzog Jewell, 'The Road to Emmaus', *Today's Christian*, July/August 2007, p. 42.
3. Ibid.
4. Ibid.
5. Andy, telephone interview by the author.
6. Ibid.
7. Dawn Herzog Jewell, 'The Road to Emmaus', op. cit., p. 44.
8. Andy, telephone interview by the author.
9. Ibid.
10. Dawn Herzog Jewell, 'The Road to Emmaus,' op. cit., p. 43.
11. In a sample of 224 male street prostitutes, 17.9 per cent identified themselves as homosexual, 46.4 per cent as heterosexual, and 35.7 per cent as bisexual. Jacqueline Boles and Kirk Elifson Kirk, 'Sexual Identity and HIV: The Male Prostitute', *The Journal of Sex Research*, 31, no.1 (1994), pp. 39–46.
12. Ibid., p. 44.
13. Ibid.
14. R. J. Valera, R. G. Sawyer and G. R. Schiraldi, 'Perceived Health Needs of Inner-City Street Prostitutes: A preliminary study', *American Journal of Health Behavior*, 25 (2001), pp. 50–59, cited in Melissa Farley and others, 'Prostitution and Trafficking in Nine Countries: An Update on Violence and Posttraumatic Stress Disorder', in *Prostitution, Trafficking and Traumatic Stress*, ed. Melissa Farley (Binghampton, New York: The Haworth Maltreatment & Trauma Press, 2003), p. 62.
15. Farley and others, op. cit., p. 62.
16. Andy, telephone interview by the author.

17. Chris McGarvey, Emmaus Ministries, printed letter, August 2006.
18. John Green, email interview by the author, 21 September 2007.
19. Melissa Farley and H. Barkan, 'Prostitution, violence and posttraumatic stress disorder', *Women & Health*, 27, no. 3 (1998), pp. 37–49, cited in Farley and others, op. cit., p. 39.
20. Sil Davis, interview by the author, Chicago, IL, 20 September 2006.
21. Paolo Cappelletti, interview by the author, São Paulo, Brazil, 12 November 2006.
22. 'São Paolo Holds Gay Pride Parade', BBC News, 11 June 2007, available online at http://news.bbc.co.uk/2/hi/americas/6738905.stm. See also http://www.globalvoices online.org/2007/06/17/gay-pride-in-brazil-35-million-march-and-government-sponsorship-in-sao-paulo/.
23. Paolo Cappelletti, interview by the author.
24. Roberto,* interview by the author, São Paolo, Brazil, 13 November 2007.
25. Ibid.
26. Christopher Kendall and Rus Ervin Funk, 'Gay Male Pornography's "Actors": When "Fantasy" Isn't', cited in *Prostitution, Trafficking and Traumatic Stress*, ed. Melissa Farley (Binghampton, New York: The Haworth Maltreatment & Trauma Press, 2003), p. 101.

Chapter 5

1. I visited the Scarlet Cord in Amsterdam on Monday, 7 May.
2. United Nations Economic Commission of Europe, 'Economic roots of trafficking in the UNECE region, fact sheet 1', 12 December 2004, cited in House Financial Services Committee, *The Sexual Gulag: Profiteering from the Global Commercial Sexual Exploitation of Women and Children*, Lisa L. Thompson, 22 June 2005.
3. Donna Hughes, *The corruption of civil society: maintaining the flow of women to the sex industries*, Encuentro Internacional Sobre Trafico De Mujeres Y

Explotacion, Andalusian Women's Institute, Malaga, Spain, 23 September 2002, cited in House Financial Services Committee, *The Sexual Gulag*, op. cit., Lisa L. Thompson.

4. Budapest Group, *The relationship between organized crime and trafficking in aliens*, Austria: International Center for Migration Policy Development, 1999, cited in House Financial Services Committee, *The Sexual Gulag*, op. cit., Lisa L. Thompson.

5. Hannah Macsween, 'Prostitution: which stance to take?' (CARE for Europe AISBL, 2007), available from http://www.care.org.uk/Publisher/File.aspx?ID=12649.

6. United Nations on Drugs and Crime, 'Trafficking in Persons', April 2006, p. 17, available online at http://www.unodc.org/pdf/traffickinginpersons_report_2006ver2.pdf.

7. US Department of State, *Trafficking in Persons Report*, June 2005, p. 6.

8. J. D'Cunha, 'Gender Equality, Human Rights and Trafficking: A Framework of Analysis and Action', paper presented at a Seminar to Promote Gender Equality and Combat Trafficking in Women and Children, Bangkok, Thailand, 7–9 October 2002, cited in *Prostitution, Trafficking and Traumatic Stress*, ed. Melissa Farley (Binghampton, New York: The Haworth Maltreatment & Trauma Press, 2003), p. 177.

9. R. Owen, 'Italy Divided Over Plan to Bring Back Brothels', 9 May 2002, available online at http://www.timesonline.co.uk/article/0,,3-290855,00.html, in *Prostitution, Trafficking and Traumatic Stress*, p. 177.

10. Donna M. Hughes, Special Issue of *Journal of International Affairs*, 'The Shadows: Promoting Prosperity or Undermining Stability?', 53, no. 2 (Spring 2000), pp. 625–51.

11. National Christian Alliance on Prostitution, 'Signpost Series 3a. Prostitution and Sex Trafficking', 1, available from: http://www.ncapuk.org/documents/signpost3d.pdf, citing *The Observer*, 18 April 2004.

12. Ibid.

13. National Christian Alliance on Prostitution, 'Signpost Series 3a. Prostitution and Sex Trafficking', 1, available from: http://www.ncapuk.org/documents/signpost3d.pdf, citing Churches Alert to Sex Trafficking across Europe, www.chaste.org.uk.

14. Home Office, *UK Action Plan on Tackling Human Trafficking*, March 2007, pp. 14–15, available from http://www.chaste.org.uk/public_documents/human-traffick-action-plan.pdf.

15. Ibid.

16. Victor Malarek, *The Natashas: Inside the New Global Sex Trade* (New York: Arcade Publishing, 2003), p. 10.

17. Ibid., pp. 13–14.

18. Christine Stark and Carol Hodgson, 'Sister Oppressions: A Comparison of Wife Battering and Prostitution', in *Prostitution, Trafficking and Traumatic Stress*, ed. Melissa Farley, op. cit., p. 22.

19. E. Giobbe, 'An Analysis of Individual, Institutional, and Cultural Pimping', *Michigan Journal of Gender and Law*, 1 (1993), pp. 33–57, cited in Christine Stark and Carol Hodgson, 'Sister Oppressions: A Comparison of Wife Battering and Prostitution', in *Prostitution, Trafficking and Traumatic Stress*, ed. Melissa Farley, op. cit., p. 19.

20. www.pimpeasybook.com.

21. Christine Stark and Carol Hodgson, 'Sister Oppressions: A Comparison of Wife Battering and Prostitution', in *Prostitution, Trafficking and Traumatic Stress*, ed. Melissa Farley, op. cit., p. 23.

22. Ibid., p. 22.

23. Cathy Zimmerman and others, *Stolen Smiles: The Physical and Psychological Health Consequences of Women and Adolescents Trafficked in Europe* (The London School of Hygiene and Tropical Medicine, 2006), summary report available from http://www.humantrafficking.org/uploads/publications/Stolen_Smiles_July_2006.pdf.

24. Christine Stark and Carol Hodgson, 'Sister Oppressions: A Comparison of Wife Battering and Prostitution,' in *Prostitution, Trafficking and Traumatic Stress*, ed. Melissa Farley, op. cit., p. 22.

25. Ibid., p. 23.
26. This excerpt was used by permission from the publisher. Fouchina Catherina, *Whom to Trust?* (Amsterdam: Oogstpublicaties, 2003), pp. 14–15.
27. Mark Wakeling, interview by the author, London, England, 9 May 2007.
28. 'For the most part, prostitution as actually practiced in the world usually does satisfy the elements of trafficking. It is rare that one finds a case in which the path to prostitution and/or a person's experiences within prostitution do not involve at least, an abuse of power and/or abuse of vulnerability' – Sigma Huda, the UN Special Rapporteur on Trafficking in Persons. United Nations Economic and Social Council, *Integration of the Human Rights of Women and a Gender Perspective: Report of the Special Rapporteur on the human rights aspects of the victims of trafficking in persons, especially, women and children*, Sigma Huda, 20 February 2006.
29. Julie Bindel, *Press for Change: A Guide for Journalists Reporting on the Prostitution and Trafficking of Women*, available from http://action.web.ca/home/catw/attach/PRESSPACKgeneric12-06.pdf.
30. Heleen Haak-de Voss, email interview by the author, 26 June 2007.
31. Toos Heemskerk-Schep, interview by the author, 7 May 2007.

Chapter 6

1. Lisa L. Thompson, telephone interview by the author, 22 May 2006.
2. National Christian Alliance on Prostitution, 'Signpost Series 3a. Prostitution and Sex Trafficking', 1; available from http://www.ncapuk.org/documents/signpost3d.pdf, citing Ward and others, 'Who Pays For Sex? An analysis of the increasing prevalence of female commercial sex contacts among men in Britain', *Sexually Transmitted Infections*, 81 (2005), pp. 467–71.

3. Nea Zoi, *Orientation Manual* (Athens, Greece, September 2005), p. 11, citing 'STOP NOW - Stop Trafficking of People' website at www.stop-trafficking.org. See also Kathy Tzilivakis, 'New Fight to Stop Sex Trade' (Hellenic Communication Service, LLC), available from http://www.helleniccomserve.com/archivedgreeknews33.html.

4. Donna Hughes, quoted in *Hands that Heal: International Curriculum to Train Caregivers of Trafficking Survivors* (draft) (Faith Alliance Against Slavery & Trafficking, 2007), p. 64.

5. American Psychological Association, *Sexualization of Girls Is Linked to Common Mental Health Problems in Girls and Women – Eating Disorders, Low Self-esteem, and Depression; an APA Task Force Reports* (press release, 19 February 2007), available from http://www.apa.org/releases/sexualization.html.

6. Ibid.

7. 'America's Most Loveable Pimp', *Rolling Stone*, 28 November 2006, available from http://www.rollingstone.com/news/coverstory/snoop_dogg_at_home_with_americas_most_lovable_pimp/page/4.

8. Willem Heemskerk, interview by the author, 7 May 2007.

9. Lyric excerpts selected from the American Psychological Association, *Report of the APA Task Force on the Sexualization of Girls* (2007), p. 7, available from http://www.apa.org/pi/wpo/sexualizationrep.pdf.

10. See http://www.sfactor.com/studios/workshops_studio.asp?location_id=2 and http://www.tri-cityherald.com/tch/life styles/life/story/9198453p-9114888c.html.

11. Regina Wang, 'Breast Augmentation Most Popular Cosmetic Surgery in United States, Study Finds', *The

California Aggie, 29 March 2007, available from
http://media.www.californiaaggie.com/media/storage/
paper981/news/2007/03/29/CityNews/Breast.Augmentat
ion. Most.Popular.Cosmetic.Surgery.In.United.States.Study.
Finds-2812058.shtml.

12. Anthony K. Valley, 'The Creepy Porn of Abercrombie
& Fitch: Are Parents Blind?' posted on 'In the Faith –
A Chronicle of the Christian Faith' website, 13
September 2003, available from http://www.inthe-
faith.com/2003/09/13/
the-creepy-porn-of-abercrombie-fitch-are-parents-
blind/.

13. Lisa Thompson, *The Normalization of Commercial Sex,
Sexual Objectification, the Rise of 'Raunch Culture'*, presentation at Vanguard University, 24 February 2007.

14. 'Bratz', Wikipedia,
http://en.wikipedia.org/wiki/Bratz.

15. American Psychological Association, *Report of the
APA Task Force on the Sexualization of Girls* (2007), p.
14, available from http://www.apa.org/pi/wpo/sex-
ualizationrep.pdf.

16. Mario Bergner, telephone interview by the author, 22
August 2007.

17. All statistics cited in the American Psychological
Association, *Report of the APA Task Force on the
Sexualization of Girls*, op. cit.

Chapter 7

1. Keith Morrison, 'Battling Sexual Addiction: Millions
of Americans Suffer from Disorder, Experts Say',
Dateline MSNBC, 24 February 2004,
http://www.msnbc.msn.com/id/
4302347/.

2. Ibid.

3. Mark Laaser, email interview by the author, 25
September 2007.

4. Keith Morrison, 'Battling Sexual Addiction', op. cit.

5. Ibid.

6. Ibid.

7. Mark Laaser, *Secret Sin: Healing the Wounds of Sexual Addiction* (Grand Rapids, MI: Zondervan, 1992), p. 13. See also the revised version, *Healing the Wounds of Sexual Addiction* (Grand Rapids, MI: Zondervan, 2004).

8. Keith Morrison, 'Battling Sexual Addiction', op. cit.

9. Mark Laaser, *The Secret Sin: Healing the Wounds of Sexual Addiction*, op. cit., p. 14.

10. Ibid., p. 17.

11. Mark Laaser, telephone interview by the author, 20 September 2007.

12. Ibid.

13. Ibid.

14. 'Pornography Statistics', Family Safe Media, http://www. familysafemedia.com/pornography_statistics.html.

15. 'What is Pornography and Sex Addiction?', Safe Families, http://www.safefamilies.org/pornaddic- tion.php.

16. 'Pornography Statistics,' Family Safe Media, op. cit.

17. Mark Laaser, telephone interview by the author.

18. American Psychological Association, *Report of the APA Task Force on the Sexualization of Girls* (2007), available from http://www.apa.org/pi/wpo/sexual- izationrep.pdf, p. 5.

19. Mark Laaser, telephone interview by the author.

20. Melissa Farley and others, 'Prostitution and Trafficking in Nine Countries: An Update on Violence and Posttraumatic Stress Disorder', in *Prostitution, Trafficking and Traumatic Stress*, ed. Melissa Farley (Binghampton, New York: The Haworth Maltreatment & Trauma Press, 2003), p. 44.

21. Christine Stark and Carol Hodgson, 'Sister Oppressions: A Comparison of Wife Battering and Prostitution', in *Prostitution, Trafficking and Traumatic Stress*, ed. Melissa Farley, op. cit., quoted in *Hands that Heal: International Curriculum to Train Caregivers of Trafficking Survivors* (draft) (Faith Alliance Against Slavery & Trafficking, 2007), p. 43.

22. Betty Rogers, 'Bitter Harvest', *Ms. Magazine*, October/November 1999, available from http://www.msmagazine.com/oct99/bitterharvest.asp.

23. Christine Stark and Carol Hodgson, 'Sister Oppressions: A Comparison of Wife Battering and Prostitution,' in Prostitution, Trafficking and Traumatic Stress, ed. Melissa Farley, op. cit., pp. 20–21.

24. 'E-sex Industry in Philippines Preys on Children', *Japan Economic Newswire*, 26 January 2005 (Lexis-Nexis), quoted in *Hands that Heal: International Curriculum to Train Caregivers of Trafficking Survivors* (draft) (Faith Alliance Against Slavery & Trafficking, 2007), p. 46.

25. Ibid.

26. Patrick Carnes, *Don't Call It Love: Recovery from Sexual Addiction* (New York: Bantam Books, 1991).

27. Mark Laaser, telephone interview by the author.

28. 'Addicted to Sex', BBC Relationships, http://www.bbc.co.uk/relationships/sex_and_sexual_health/probs_sex addiction.shtml.

29. Ibid.

30. Ibid.

31. Mark Laaser, telephone interview by the author.

32. Mark Laaser, *Secret Sin: Healing the Wounds of Sexual Addiction*, op. cit., p. 15.

33. Ibid.

34. Ibid., p. 23.

35. Mario Bergner, telephone interview by the author, 22 August 2007.

36. Jerry Ropelato, 'Internet Pornography Statistics', Top Ten Reviews, www.internet-filter-review.toptenreviews.com. internet-pornography-statistics.html.

37. Jill,* telephone interview by the author, 16 August 2007.

Chapter 8

1. Excerpt from Myrto Theocharous, 'Kidnapped', unpublished paper, www.iteams.org (14 March 2007).

2. Eirini Chatzigiani, conversation with the author, Athens, Greece, 30 April 2007.

3. Nea Zoi, *Orientation Manual*, p. 19.
4. Ibid., p. 18.
5. Ibid., p. 3.
6. Myrto Theocharous, interview by the author, Wheaton, IL, 7 December 2006.
7. Ibid.
8. Ibid.
9. Ibid.
10. Dina Petrou, telephone interview by the author, 5 May 2007.
11. Ibid.

Chapter 9

1. Jennifer Roemhildt, interview by the author, 4 May 2007.
2. Nea Zoi, *Orientation Manual* (Athens, Greece, September 2005), p. 21.
3. Ibid., p. 5, citing 'STOP NOW - Stop Trafficking of People' website at www.stop-trafficking.org.
4. Nea Zoi, *Orientation Manual*, op. cit., p. 5.
5. Ibid., p. 11, citing 'STOP NOW - Stop Trafficking of People' website at www.stop-trafficking.org. See also Kathy Tzilivakis, 'New Fight to Stop Sex Trade' (Hellenic Communication Service, L.L.C.), available from http://www. helleniccomserve.com/archivedgreeknews33.html.
6. Nea Zoi, *Orientation Manual*, op. cit., p. 10.
7. Mary,* interview by the author, Athens, Greece, 4 May 2007.
8. Nea Zoi, *Orientation Manual*, op. cit., p. 12.
9. Ibid.
10. Ibid., p. 15.
11. Ibid., p. 10.
12. Emma Skjonsby Manousaridou, interview by the author, 3 May 2007.
13. Jennifer Roemhildt, interview by the author, 4 May 2007.
14. Jorgen Carling, 'Trafficking in Women from Nigeria to Europe' (International Peace Research Institute,

Oslo, 1 July 2005), http://www.migrationinformation.org/Feature/display.cfm?id=318.
15. Ibid.
16. Ibid.
17. Ibid.
18. Nea Zoi, *Orientation Manual*, op. cit., p. 8.

Chapter 10

1. Harmony Dust, telephone interview by the author.
2. Harmony Dust, interview by Dean Curry.
3. Harmony Dust, telephone interview by the author.
4. Treasures, *Training Manual* (Los Angeles, CA).
5. Ibid., p. 11.
6. Ibid., p. 14.
7. Ibid.
8. Harmony Dust, telephone interview by the author.
9. Harmony Dust, email to the author, 19 September 2007.
10. Sheila Weller, 'No one Should Have to Be a Stripper', *Glamour*, January 2007, p. 177.
11. Ibid.
12. Harmony Dust, email to the author.
13. Edna,* telephone interview by the author, 26 January 2007.
14. Edna, email, 10 August 2007.
15. Edna, email, 19 September 2007.

Chapter 11

1. This chapter was first in Dawn Herzog Jewell, 'The Road to Emmaus', *Today's Christian*, July/August 2007.
2. John Green, email to the author, 19 September 2007.

Chapter 12

1. Roberto,* interview by the author, 18 November 2007.
2. Sil Davis, interview by the author.

3. Nea Zoi, *Volunteer Manual*, p. 12.
4. Ibid., p. 13.
5. Myrto Theocharous, interview by the author.

Chapter 13

1. Gatheredvoices.com provides a space for people who have felt excluded to have a voice. The website compiles writings, stories and images created primarily by people who have been exploited through prostitution or sex trafficking. 'Forgiveness' was used by permission. Available from: http://www.gatheredvoices.com/index.php?option=com_content&task=view&id=40&Itemid=55.
2. Kathy Stout-LaBauve, telephone interview by the author, 27 March 2007.
3. Thelma Nambu, interview by the author, Manila, Philippines, 20 February 2006.
4. 'From the lips of children and infants you have ordained praise because of your enemies, to silence the foe and the avenger' (Psalm 8:2).
5. Pierre Tami, telephone interview by the author, 31 October 2006.

Chapter 14

1. Estelle Blake, interview by the author, London, England, 10 May 2007.
2. Thelma Nambu, interview by the author, Manila, Philippines, 20 February 2006.
3. Jonathan Nambu, email interview by the author, 19 September 2007.
4. Edna Vallenilla, interview by the author, Amsterdam, Netherlands, 7 May 2007.

Chapter 15

1. Julia,* interview by the author, São Paolo, Brazil, 18 November 2006.

2. Renata Bortoleto, Ana Laura Diniz and Michele Izawa, *Contes de Bordel* (São Paolo, Brazil: Carrenho Editorial, 2003), pp. 23–27.
3. Ibid., p. 21.
4. National Christian Alliance on Prostitution, 'A Good Practice Guide: for local community projects supporting individuals involved in prostitution to offer freedom and change' (draft) (London, England, 2007), p. 12.
5. Ibid.
6. Nea Zoi, *Orientation Manual* (Athens, Greece, September 2005), pp. 13–14, citing Door of Hope, *Induction Manual*.
7. Nea Zoi, *Orientation Manual*, op. cit., p. 15.
8. Laura Coulterer, 'Portrait of Exploitation', *Prism*, September/October 2007, p. 11.
9. Ibid., p. 10.
10. Mary Raynovich, telephone interview by the author, 31 May 2006.
11. Ibid.
12. Ibid.
13. Ibid.
14. Used by permission. GatheredVoices.com, http://www.gatheredvoices.com/index.php?option=com_content&task=view&id=16&Itemid=55

Chapter 16

1. This chapter was first published in Dawn Herzog Jewell, 'Red-light Rescue', *Christianity Today*, January 2007.
2. Kerry Hilton, email to the author, 27 September 2007.
3. Read more about Business as Mission from Mats Tunehag at http://www.businessasmission.com/pages/papers_articles.

Chapter 17

1. Bevs, interview with the author, Manila, Philippines, 20 February 2006.
2. Ibid.

3. Bevs, interview with Thelma Nambu, 2 November 2005.
4. Bevs, interview with the author, Manila, Philippines, 20 February 2006.
5. Jonathan Nambu, interview with the author, 20 February 2006.
6. Sil Davis, interview with the author.
7. Pierre Tami, telephone interview with the author, 31 October 2006.
8. Amy Durkee, 'Sophia's Circle: Healing Through Friendship, Sisterhood, Faith', *Prism*, September/October 2007, p. 14.
9. Ibid., p. 15.
10. Ibid.
11. Ana, interview with the author.

Chapter 18

1. Jennifer Roemhildt, interview by the author.
2. Lauran Bethell, 'Discerning Your Call', presentation at Vanguard University conference, 'Strategies Against Sex Trafficking', Los Angeles, California, 24 February 2007.
3. Josephine Wakeling, email interview by the author, 24 September 2007.
4. Eileen,* interview by the author, London, England, 10 May 2007.
5. Dr. Beth Grant, plenary presentation at Vanguard University conference, 'Strategies Against Sex Trafficking', Los Angeles, California, 24 February 2007.
6. Ruth Robb and Marion Carson, *Working the Streets: A Handbook for Christians Involved in Outreach to Prostitutes* (Chichester, UK: New Wine Press, 2002), p. 36.
7. Jennifer Roemhildt, interview by the author.
8. Dr Beth Grant, telephone interview by the author, 1 March 2007.

Chapter 19

1. Jamelyn Lederhouse, interview by the author, 6 January 2007.
2. Mark Crawford, telephone interview by the author.
3. Toos Heemskerk-Schep, interview by the author, 7 May 2007.
4. Jonathan Nambu, interview by the author.
5. Estelle Blake, interview by the author.
6. Eileen,* interview by the author, 10 May 2007.
7. Dr Beth Grant, telephone interview by the author.
8. The Baptist Union of Sweden, http://www.samverkanmot trafficking.se/english.asp.
9. Project Rescue, http://www.projectrescue.com/1/1purpose.php.
10. Dr. Beth Grant, telephone interview by the author.
11. Ibid.

Chapter 20

1. Kelly, used by permission.
2. Jonathan Nambu, email interview by the author.
3. Harmony Dust, telephone interview by the author.
4. Alex Jones-Moreno, telephone interview by the author, 18 September 2007.
5. Josephine Wakeling, email to the author, 21 September 2007.

Chapter 21

1. Salvation Army Prayer Guide available at http://www.salvationarmyusa.org/usn/www_usn.nsf/0/2BC5E765DD 1AEBD98025733D005C1954/$file/Prayer%20Guide%20-%20plain.pdf
2. www.salvationarmyusa.org/trafficking.
3. Mark 5:21–43; Luke 8:40–56.